AWAKENING TO AWE

AWAKENING TO AWE

PERSONAL STORIES OF
PROFOUND TRANSFORMATION

Kirk J. Schneider

JASON ARONSON
Lanham • Boulder • New York • Toronto • Plymouth, UK

Published in the United States of America
by Jason Aronson
An imprint of Rowman & Littlefield Publishers, Inc.

A wholly owned subsidiary of
The Rowman & Littlefield Publishing Group, Inc.
4501 Forbes Boulevard, Suite 200, Lanham, Maryland 20706
www.rowmanlittlefield.com

Estover Road
Plymouth PL6 7PY
United Kingdom

British Library Cataloguing in Publication Information Available

Library of Congress Cataloging-in-Publication Data

Schneider, Kirk J.
  Awakening to awe : personal stories of profound transformation / Kirk J.
Schneider.— 1st ed.
      p. cm.
  Includes bibliographical references and index.
  ISBN 978-0-7657-0664-5 (cloth : alk. paper)
  ISBN 978-0-7657-0665-2 (pbk. : alk. paper)
  ISBN 978-0-7657-0666-9 (electronic)
  1. Awe. 2. Mystery. I. Title.
  BF575.A9S35 2009
  155.2'5—dc22   2009013977

Printed in the United States of America

∞ ™ The paper used in this publication meets the minimum requirements of
American National Standard for Information Sciences—Permanence of Paper
for Printed Library Materials, ANSI/NISO Z39.48-1992.

To William James and Rollo May:
Torchbearers for mystery

CONTENTS

CONTENTS

PREFACE

How often do we hear young people today exclaim, "That's awe-some!" Or, "I'm in awe?" Or in another context, how often do we hear military authorities characterize their bombing operations in the quasi-apocalyptic terms "shock and awe"? A bit too often, I'm afraid. Yet the fact that "awe"—and its variants—is flooding our vocabulary is not an altogether menacing sign. Indeed it is perhaps a welcoming sign that beyond its casual usage, the fuller and deeper sensibility of "awe" is reemerging in our culture.

Despite this hope, the sensibility of awe has undergone many incarnations in humanity's history. In ancient times, for example, awe was viewed quite narrowly as the sense of being daunted or overcome, particularly by nature. The experience of being daunted, as Rudolf Otto put it in his classic study of religion, *The Idea of the Holy*,[1] was the primal experience of creation, and the primal experience of creation, he went on, was the seedbed for religion. On the other hand, in more recent years, the sensibility of awe has either been neglected, as was the case during the industrial revolution and rise of science, or in our contemporary age, embraced mainly for its exalting qualities, such as its capacity to thrill.

The truth, however, is that awe is neither a paralyzing jolt nor a "feel good" boost but a profound and complex *attitude*. This attitude, for those fortunate enough to harbor it, embraces *both* apprehension and thrill, humility and the grandeur of creation. Hence when young people proclaim "awwwesome," they often appear to glimpse but not necessarily embrace essential awe.

This book then provides a counterbalance to such one-sided—and hence devitalized—expressions of awe. Through both reflection and narrative this book shows how we can meld the best of our ancestral traditions (e.g., humility, depth, and formality) with the finest of our modernistic tendencies (e.g., boldness, spontaneity, and openness) to forge a renewed path for humanity.

In particular, this book highlights the nature and power of awe to transform lives. In this sense, it is akin to other self-help guides but with one major difference: the emphasis on people's "living" stories. For example, readers will discover how awe transformed the life of an ex-gang member, Jim Hernandez, into a beloved and productive youth educator; an ex-drug addict, Michael Cooper, into a communally conscious healer; and a sufferer of stage-three cancer, E. Mark Stern, into a contemplative and spiritual seeker. The book will also inform readers about the challenges and joys of awe-based child-rearing, education, humor, political activism, and aging. Drawing on the philosophy of my earlier work, the acclaimed *Rediscovery of Awe*,[2] *Awakening to Awe* tells the down-to-earth stories of a quiet yet emerging movement. This movement requires neither religion nor formulas, neither pills nor wealth, but an approach to life, natural and free to all.

That which I call "awe-based awakening," then, is not simply an inheritance but must be realized and cultivated.

Below is a preview of the core conditions—both favorable and unfavorable—to the cultivation of awe-based awakening. This preview based on the testimonies of contributors to the book will give the reader a sampling of the remarkable insights to be revealed.

I. CONDITIONS THAT *FAVOR* AWE-BASED AWAKENING (OR THE HUMILITY AND WONDER— AMAZEMENT—OF LIVING):

- A basic capacity to subsist
- The time to reflect

- A capacity to slow down
- A capacity to savor the moment
- A focus on what one loves
- A capacity to see the big picture
- An openness to the mystery of life and being
- An appreciation for the fact of life
- An appreciation of pain as a sometime teacher
- An appreciation of balance (e.g., between one's fragility and resiliency)
- Contemplative time alone
- Contemplative time in natural or non-distracting settings
- Contemplative time with close friends or companions
- In-depth therapy or meditation
- An ability to stay present to and accept the evolving nature of conflict (e.g., to know that "this too shall pass")
- An ability to stay present to and accept the evolving nature of life
- An ability to give oneself over—discerningly—to the ultimately unknowable
- An ability to trust in the ultimately unknowable

II. CONDITIONS *UNFAVORABLE* TO AWE-BASED AWAKENING (OR THE HUMILITY AND WONDER—AMAZEMENT—OF LIVING):

- Poverty and deprivation
- Haste
- Rigidity
- Dogma
- Gluttony
- Anarchy
- Self-inflation
- Self-deflation
- The preoccupation with money
- The preoccupation with status

- The preoccupation with consumerism
- A steady diet of junk food, pills, or alcohol
- A steady diet of mind-numbing TV
- An enthrallment with mechanization
- An enthrallment with simple answers
- A compulsion to think positively
- A compulsion to think negatively
- Fixation
- Coercion
- Reductionism
- Polarization

In closing, my deepest appreciation to all the brave souls who have graced this volume, and by so doing, graced life itself.

INTRODUCTION
Awe-Wakening

The blocking of one's capacity for wonder and the loss of the capacity to appreciate mystery can have serious effects upon our . . . health, not to mention the health of our whole planet.

—Rollo May, *Dialogues: Therapeutic Applications of Existential Philosophy*

To know that what is impenetrable to us really exists, manifesting itself as the highest wisdom and the most radiant beauty, which our dull faculties can comprehend only in the most primitive forms—this knowledge, this feeling, is at the center of true religiousness. In this sense, and in this sense only, I belong to the ranks of the devoutly religious.

—Albert Einstein, *What I Believe*

Fifty years ago, when I was two and a half, I lost my seven-year-old brother to a disease of the heart. Thirty-four years ago, when I was eighteen, I lost my uncle to a massive heart attack; and then my father, five years later, to the same malady.

Since then, I have lived in this very selective mystery. The doctors have all assured me that I'm doing all one can. I take the right pills, eat the right foods, and exercise—but still (and naturally, I believe), I wonder.

There have been three times in my life when I've been scared out of my wits. The first time was after my brother died, and I unraveled. I'd sob for hours in the dark, and retreat to a paralyzing world.

The second major time was when I was about fifteen and almost drowned in the ocean. A pulverizing storm had arisen just fifty miles off the coast of Virginia. Daredevils that my father and I were, we plunged into that storm and tried to surf its unruly waves. The result was a bone-crushing brush with oblivion.

The third time was when I was in graduate school (a long way from home) and was challenged (by a revered professor) to work with psychotic patients. Shortly thereafter, I saw a terrifying movie about psychosis, which, in turn, precipitated a kind of psychosis in me, and a months-long rehabilitation.

I convey these episodes, not to elicit sympathy from the reader, but to illustrate a point: following each one of these upheavals, I learned something crucial about awe. The first thing I learned is that no matter how desperate I got, no matter how warped and whipped by mystery, I did not need to extinguish mystery. I needed neither pills nor dogma to contort it. Not to say that I was some kind of superman, impervious to hurt; quite the contrary. I took some desperate measures on occasion and erected my own barriers against mystery—among these, escapism, denial, and withdrawal.

However, in the long run, and with the help of some profoundly healing encounters, I realized that the answer lay not in the neutralizing but in the illuminating; not in the resolving but in the venturing. In these ways, change and the unknown gradually became portals—openings for awareness. Among these openings was a jarring yet deepened sense of the temporariness of life, and the value of the moment in its wake; another was the discovery of solitude and the play, creativity and wonder that often sprung from it; another was the abrupt realization of life's uncertainties, and the gradual shift from fear to intrigue in the face of them. This latter sensibility was especially acute in my fascination for science fiction. I would spend many absorbing hours either creating or watching stories about distant lands, outer space, or peculiar states of mind. I would be unnerved by these scenarios but also and equally enthralled. Books such as *The Phantom Tollbooth, A Wrinkle in Time,* and *The Fall of the House of Usher*; movies such as *The Wizard of Oz, To Kill a Mockingbird,* and *Frankenstein*; and TV shows such as *The Outer Limits, One Step Beyond,* and *The Twilight Zone* became my intimate companions. I could lie on my bedroom floor for perhaps hours, following a dramatic show, or even an intense sob, and make up characters, plays, and ideas for movies. I even made up a play movie studio, complete with "contract players," scripts, drawings, and toy sets. As I got older, these forays morphed into short-story writing, poetry, and an impassioned interest in philosophy and psychology. In sum, I became fascinated by existence and the grand questions of existence—who are we, what are we, and what is being all about? I was not so much directed to these questions as supported to discover them, wrestle with their implications, and follow out their leads. This was not an easy road, to be sure—nor a linear one—but it was, ultimately, a rewarding one; for I—like a growing number of fellow strugglers today—found solace in mystery.

This book is a testament to the solace of mystery (amazement) as distinct from the solace of pat answers or pills that we so often content ourselves with today. On the pages to follow, I assemble a cadre of people whose lives are an avowal to the healing and transformative power of awe. The people I have assembled in this book agree: the old remedies of dogmatic religion (obsession, absolutism, idolatry) and the new remedies of drug-taking (or drug-like reprogramming), while helpful at times as a palliative, are just not the enduring solution for many people. We have had too many wars, breakdowns, and disillusionments in their wake.

Hence, it is time for something new to emerge in our culture, and indeed world, if we are to save ourselves as a species. And that something, to those of us congregated in this volume, is integrally connected to awe.

THE NATURE AND POWER OF AWE

It is ever there, awaiting.

It is not *about* God but *beyond* God—an ever-flowing fount.

The awesomeness of life, of being, is inexhaustible. No matter what we lose, fear, or despise, it is there. It is there at our darkest hour, in trial as in devastation, in life as in death, because it is beyond life and death, trial and devastation.

It's not that it is readily accessible, perceivable, or even conceivable; at our worst times, it is opaque.

However, it is *available*, and that availability can be realized in an instant or a lifetime.

Awe is the God beyond God, the origin and the destination, the expanding question and the expanding answer.[1] It is our humility and wonder before creation; our astonishment before creation.[2] Awe is neither the bliss-filled light nor the despair-riddled dark—it is the MORE—whether bliss-filled or desperate.

Awe connects us with creation. But not the creation of commandments; the creation of amazement, vastness.

Awe is our fundamental connection to mystery—vastness, amazement; it is the deliverance of the locked-in soul and the balm of the tireless adventurer.

Within the sheen of awe, the destination becomes the journey and the journey the destination. There is no place to "get to"; there is ever a place to "be with," revel in, and tremble before. As soon as we try to freeze it, we've lost it; as soon as we endeavor to skirt it, we've cheated it.

The power is in the paradox: terror yet wonder, uncertainties yet majesties.

Our task is to mine the terrors and wonders, uncertainties and majesties—to question with reverence, and to revere our questions.

Renowned religious authority Karen Armstrong says something similar about the need for what she terms "mystical agnosticism." She notes that the world has witnessed the debacles of fundamentalist tyrannies, and equally, of post-enlightenment oligarchies, and that the God of the mystics might . . . present a possible alternative. . . . This God is in tune with the atheistic mood of our secular society. . . . Even if we are incapable of the higher states of consciousness achieved by a mystic, we can learn that God does not exist in any simplistic sense, for example, or that the very word "God" is only a symbol of a reality that ineffably transcends it. The mystical agnosticism could help us to acquire a restraint that stops us rushing into . . . complex matters with dogmatic assurance.[3]

In the passages to follow, then, I will trace the stories of people who venerate the questions of life, and who bring that gratitude to common human challenges, from the negotiation of trauma and illness, to the education of children, to the triumph of sobriety and humor. Each story is a story of personal awakening ("awe-wakening"), but each is also a story of societal awakening—indeed of the awakening of humanity—if only we could but heed the lessons foretold. Put concretely, each story provides an alternative to the desperate and desolate remedies that are so prevalent today, from religious platitudes to medical palliatives. And each provides a glimpse into what cultural anthropologist Ernest Becker has called "a community of the abandoned."

The human being, writes Becker,

is the only animal who senses that he might have been abandoned on this planet. . . . I think this level of awareness might have something in it of a destiny of man, that at his highest point of personal liberation from the constraints of others and of culture, he comes face to face with the problem of the meaning of all life. And, having come to this, that he can find no secure answer or hope, but only a yearning that has in it elements of both love and despair. Perhaps it is only at this point that one can speak of an authentic religious consciousness for our time, much as the Psalms represented such a consciousness for an earlier time.[4]

I

OUR AWE-DEPLETED AGE

efore we present the stories of our contributors to this volume, we need to address, by way of background, one overarching question—what keeps so many of us from "awe-wakening?" What keeps so many of us from discovering, let alone finding, awe-based paths?

Awe is our fundamental relationship to mystery—how did this fundamental relationship get so warped? How did a basic sense of life, the grandeur and amazement—chill and thrill—of existing, become either the plaything of egotists or the prison of cynics, the crippler of dreamers or the seducer of tyrants?

How is it that we can *feel*—from our first breath perhaps—a wealth of life, love, and possibility, and yet spurn and minimize these sensibilities at every turn?

How is it that the vast and inexhaustible fascinations of life get so ignored, denied, and despised—and the disdainful and sometimes violent world we know emerges?

The truth is that from the instant we are born, we are stunned by mystery. We are stunned by mystery's unpredictability, disorientation, and even splendor. From a certain standpoint, this makes exquisite sense. From the moment we can taste, touch, see, and hear, for example, we flounder. While some of this floundering is tolerable, fairly rapidly it needs to be quelled and organized so that we can meet elemental needs. This is what we call "enculturation,"

and some degree of enculturation—or diversion from mystery—is
essential to our survival.

The problem, however, is that quite rapidly we not only need
"some degree" of diversion from the splendor and anxiety, or in
short, awe, of our worlds, we need (in our culture, at least) to repel
many of these qualities utterly. To form a culture like ours, a culture predicated on the avoidance of disarray, we need to cultivate
intricate defenses against mystery, and to acquire sophisticated
strategies that enable us to skirt the complexities of being. Hence,
much of our speech is geared not to acknowledge our humility before life, but our control, coordination, and management of life. Our
relations become predicated not on our capacities for wonder and
exploration, but on our inclinations toward convenience, haste, and
regimentation.

But the neglect of our fundamental relationship to mystery does
not end there. Not by any means. The enculturation part is prob-
lematic enough with regard to savoring of mystery, but compound-
ing this situation is the thornier challenge of human crisis. What
happens to our sense of the humility and wonder of living—the
vastness of living—when we encounter an incomprehensible loss,
ailment, or disruption? What happens when we are jarred from our
routine, as resilient as that routine may be—when we are flailing,
desperate, askew?

What can happen are two basic prospects: we turn toward a fix
(e.g., a leader, a religion, or a drug) for our salvation, or we turn
toward a path of inner (and outer) transformation, healing, and
recovery. A path toward awe.

This book is about the growing cadre of seekers who embrace an
"awe-based" view of life. By awe-based, I mean a take on life that
embraces *both* the wonders of existence *and* the human responsibility to engage, discern, and ethically respond to those wonders. To
bring this down to earth, I'm talking about people who are looking
beyond the quick-fix model of living today—whether that model
shows up in the things we buy, religious salvation, or a psychiatric
pill.

There is an emerging generation of people who realize that human beings are complex creatures, and that a one-size-fits-all solution is not the answer; on the other hand, they also realize that no matter which way you go, you can't have it all, and there will invariably be need for compromise. The question is, where do we compromise? For how long? And with what measure of loss? These are increasingly pressing matters.

1

WHAT KEEPS US FROM VENTURING?

To give readers a sense of the depth of our awe-based depletion, I am fond of imparting the following parable:

What if I told you that *you* are about to embark on a "great adventure,"[1] and that you are about to be given all the proper equipment for this adventure—food, shelter, clothing?

And what if I told you further that you are about to experience the terrors and wonders of the cosmos on this journey, that you will meet a wide array of beings—both human and nonhuman—along the way, and that every day you will have a chance to marvel at, be moved by, and imagine an entirely new way to live?

And finally, here is the real clincher: what if I told you that you'd have about eight decades to fulfill this journey, and that following those roughly eighty years, you would embark on an even *more* fascinating and enigmatic trek?

Would you want to go?

Would you cherish every moment of the opportunity, and gather up all your strength to participate?

And given these remarkable anticipations, would you have any inclinations to devalue, exploit, or even kill yourself or others along the way?

Would you have any desire to trim, skim, or dodge what you experience? Or to prettify, package, or replace it?

Maybe, but it is unlikely.

And yet here we are, a couple of hundred thousand years of humanity, and still, as a whole, negligent of our great adventure—bathed in denial, snared by greed, and numbed by indifference. We are bedeviled by illusions, be they of guns, gimmicks, or gods.

How is it that we are so derailed, especially today?

HAPPINESS VS. DEPTH

Even in periods of national distress, comprehensive surveys extol the happiness, if not outright elation, of the American people. A recent poll in *Time* magazine (2005), for example, reported that 78 percent of Americans are happy, and then on its cover announced: "The science of happiness: Why optimists live longer. . . ."[2] But let us take a closer look at these results. Many people who are happy, that is, more satisfied with life, according to these surveys, also appear to be the very same people who, according to another body of research, tend to be self-inflated, image-conscious, and conformist, and intellectually as well as emotionally inert.[3] Correlatively, this same research shows that mildly to moderately depressed individuals, and particularly those who have suffered but subsequently overcome their depression, tend to be (1) more realistic about life, (2) possess more tolerance of intellectual and cultural diversity, and (3) show a superior ability to psychologically grow, relative to the happy population.[4]

Hence what does it really mean to be a "happy and optimistic" people in our time? What does it mean to feel "good" about life and the acquisitions of life? Does it mean, for example, that one becomes less prone to stress because one steeps oneself in the high-tech isolation of an iPod, a cell phone, or a computer chat room? Does it mean that one buries oneself in routines, overeats, and consumes copious amounts of alcohol? Does it mean that one indulges in mood-altering pills or seeks immediate salvation? Does it mean that one confines oneself to a rigid but reassuring set of moral values, or a tight-knit community of worship? Does it mean that one turns one's life into sports channel installments or encampments at the local mall? Does it mean that one becomes a smooth social operator who can charm and manipulate at will?

As strident as these questions may seem, and some are admittedly provocative, are they so far-fetched? What else could it mean that happier people, as previously indicated, also show relatively greater tendencies toward narrow-mindedness, hedonism, and complacency than less happy people?

The research also implies that there are some very curious overlaps in our culture between what is considered normal and happiness. For example, if most Americans are happy, then what are we to make of other findings regarding large segments of our population: To wit, the polls that indicate that nearly six out of ten Americans believe that the prophesies in the book of Revelation (such as the Rapture and a war with Islam) are going to come true;[5] or that nearly one quarter of the U.S. population "believe that using violence to get what they want is acceptable";[6] or that Americans now spend more on gambling than on movies, DVDs, music, and books combined;[7] or that 67 percent of U.S. men and 57 percent of U.S. women are overweight or obese.[8]

Could it be that regimentation, absolutism, and uncritical nationalism, on the one hand, or materialism, opportunism, and gluttony, on the other, are the new standards of "well-adjusted" living?

Something still does not jibe here. Something does not jibe when I turn on the evening news night after night (particularly in the years leading up to the 2008 presidential election) to find that many "happy" people have supported a government that shuns dialogue and glorifies military superiority, that coddles billionaires and ignores or trivializes minimum-wage earners, teachers, and educators, not to mention the healthcare system and quality job training. Something is off base when a majority of voters endorse a political leadership that snubs treaties on global warming, dismantles decades of clean air legislation and environmental protection laws, and subverts scientific scrutiny of the pharmaceutical industry.[9] Something is awry regarding the state of normalcy in this country when a significant majority in Congress endorses candidates for attorney general and ambassador to the United Nations, respectively, who associate with the sanctioning of torture at U.S. military prisons (or their satellites) and express contempt for the very institution that is about to be served.[10] There is a scary disconnect about the relative robust support for an administration that spends lavishly to engage in government-sponsored, yet journalistically packaged, self-promotional advertising,[11] and that permits its highest military leaders to maintain their positions in the face of withering military disasters, such as the Abu Ghraib scandal, the neglect of intelligence data leading up to 9/11, and the loss of thousands of lives following the fall of Baghdad due to poor postwar planning.[12] Finally, it is difficult to square the endorsement of a leadership that forfeits its regulatory power to corrupt captains of industry who associate with the largest financial collapse since the Great Depression.[13]

Could it be that what conventional psychology calls life satisfaction in this country is, in part, an exercise in collective sleepwalking? Could it be that what the popular press calls American happiness is a seductive but disturbing delusion?

Granted, these contradictions in the exercise of human happiness, health, and so on have sharply intensified in the wake of the 9/11 disaster. Our country had a reason to be in some degree of denial, and to base a portion of our lives on fear-driven palliatives; but the problem goes much deeper than the 9/11 disaster. It goes to the whole question of living well, of health. What is health, if not to be whole and supple and free? What is satisfaction if not to be gratified in the deepest fibers of our being, to live fully, with as few consolations to fashion, artifice, and dogma as possible? What is well-being but the expansion of honesty, awareness, and grit—to call life as one sees it, and to absorb life as one meets it?

What is joy but *engagement*, the maximal encounter with the challenges and opportunities of life—and my, how we have failed to engage as a people, though we have inured ourselves with comforts.

Freedom, which is intimately connected to happiness, is also a much-trumpeted term these days. President Bush used it in his 2005 State of the Union speech twenty-eight times! But what does he, or the mentality he represents, really mean by the stress on freedom?

My concern is that too frequently it means expediency—the quickest, cheapest, easiest way to conduct our lives. This portrait of freedom is all about us today—a preemptive war in Iraq, deploying massive amounts of arms and personnel to radically revamp the Middle East in our own (capitalist) image, above and beyond, it appears, the question of what interests the indigenous people; a vigorously unfettered marketplace where investment and capital can move about virtually unchecked; a quasi-regulated drug industry; an easily digestible moral code to uphold these "freedoms"; and so on.

But freedom is more than external gratification, it is more than satisfaction of appetites, or fulfillments of prophesies.

FIDDLING WHILE ROME BURNS:
THE "ANSWER"-DRIVEN LIFE

Freedom is also—and perhaps foremost—an inner condition: the capacity to pause, to reflect, and to discern. The fashionable view of freedom is not encompassing of these dimensions, or barely so. A case in point is the wildly popular book *The Purpose-Driven Life* (2002) by Rick Warren.[14] This book—which has sold more than twenty million copies worldwide—is an articulate, highly accessible guide to finding happiness, fulfillment, and freedom through biblical edict. The chief message of the book, that our possibilities are so much more than the petty conflicts and difficulties of our day-to-day lives, is a majestic one. It inspires prisoners to reform, and CEO's to become moralists, but what really is the "take-home" instruction? It is this: that to find happiness one needs to adopt Jesus (God) into one's heart, methodically read and follow scriptures, and regularly attend church. Hence, the purpose-driven life, according to this book, is a pietistic life. It is a life of emancipation from finite day-to-day difficulties, for example, with friends, coworkers, illnesses and the like, through the adoption of God, as that is defined in the Christian Bible.

But what is that deity that is defined in the Christian Bible, or any religious testament for that matter? It is a source of inviolable standards, an authority, that indeed transforms, but does it really free, particularly if freedom is defined not by outer dictates, but by inner choices, allowances? While some may protest that biblical beliefs are freely chosen, the question is to what extent, and to what extent is the choosing permitted to be maintained? Too often, within very narrow parameters, it appears, because "answers" are inviolable.

Nevertheless, the protest will continue: biblical beliefs do make people feel happier, and they enrich many lives.

No doubt this is true, and we see the fruits of it every day in rehab centers, hospitals, and houses of worship; but the question remains, at what price, and with what long-term individual and collective consequences? No matter how convincing the message, the Bible (or for that matter, any valued life-philosophy) can only be restorative to the extent that it permits inquiry, dialogue, and revision. It is only truly replenishing to the degree that it enables a living, evolving vision. Short of that, the teaching becomes a dictate, an oppressor, and a sham—the very opposite of what it had intended to be.

Hence, democracy can be a sham if it is imposed on a people without their consent. Happiness, tolerance, and even love can become falsehoods if they are proffered without awareness of any of the other emotions or contexts that may challenge, add to, or embellish them—such as the acknowledgment of economic injustice, the questioning of military power, or the cognizance of prejudice.

In this light, I am cautiously optimistic that, in part due to our reaction *against* the recent debacles, we now have a leader—Barack Obama—who recognizes the multifaceted nature of human liberation. My hope is that he sees the need for depth as well as breadth, humility as well as farsightedness, in the conduct of our personal and collective affairs.

The challenge today, then, is to overcome our quick-fix, single-answer infatuation. *It is not a question of disavowing faith or happiness or democracy, it is a question of disavowing the hype and gimmickry that too often attend these time-honored virtues and that divert us from a more substantive engagement.*

2

THE STODGY
ROAD TO AWE

In 1974, cultural anthropologist and academic lightning rod Ernest Becker lay dying in a hospital room when a perceptive young reporter from *Psychology Today* magazine, Sam Keen, began a remarkable interview. Becker was just forty-nine years old and the recipient of the Pulitzer Prize for literature for his groundbreaking work, *The Denial of Death*, and the irony was not lost on Keen.

"I realize this morning I held you at arm's length," Keen remarked toward the end of his inquiry with Becker. "My attitude was a perfect illustration of your thesis about the denial of death. I wanted to exile you in a category from which I was excluded—namely, the dying. That is human enough but silly because it prevents me from asking you some questions . . ."[1]

Keen goes on, "You have thought as hard about death as anybody I know. And now, as it were, you are doing your empirical research. . . . And somehow, I would like to ask you what you can add now that you are closer to [the] experience?"[2]

Becker pauses a moment, then relates,

I see what you mean. . . . I would say that the most important thing is to know that beyond the absurdity of one's own life, beyond the human viewpoint, beyond what is happening to us, is the fact of the tremendous creative energies of the cosmos that are using us for some purposes we don't know. To be used for divine purposes, however we may be misused, this is the thing that consoles. . . . I think one . . . should try to just hand over one's life, the meaning of it, the end of it. This has been the most important to me.[3]

With this statement, Becker—an avowed scientist, Enlightenment thinker, and secularist—embraces faith, albeit of the most demanding kind. For although Becker "gives himself over" to creation, it is in an exceptional form—very different from the reflexive surrender to which we have alluded, but exalted, replenishing, and even joyous nonetheless. As Becker states elsewhere, this giving over is a hard-fought conscious one, not a simple bow to salvation, or the "ready at hand." It is a giving up "when there's nothing left," after a lifetime of study, discovery, and self-creation. To this extent, Becker embodies the best of both worlds: passion in life, and hope in the "complex" mystery of death.[4]

The road to awe—the humility and wonder, and splendor and mystery of living—is a rousing and dynamic one. There is no short-cut to awe. One needs grit and openness to partake of its fruits. Awe embraces the whole of life, the fearsome and the fascinating, the frail and far ranging. Death, despair, and pathos are all integral to awe, as are blitheness and joy. The poignancy of life, the mead of life, these are the keynotes of the awe-informed course.

Whitman knew this well:

> Great is goodness: I do not know what it is any more than I know what health is . . . but I know it is great. Great is wickedness. . . . Do you call that a paradox? It certainly is a paradox.
> The eternal equilibrium of things is great, and the eternal overthrow of things is great. And there is another paradox. Great is life . . . and real and mystical . . . wherever and whoever. Great is death. . . . Sure as life holds all parts together, death holds all parts together; Sure as the stars return again after they merge in the light, death is great as life.[5]

OBJECTIVE UNCERTAINTY, HELD FAST

Giving up when there's nothing left—at the very apex of one's powers—and taking the leap into the "tremendous creative energies of the cosmos" as opposed to a static truth or answer or God, is also the province of another critical thinker of the post-Enlightenment era, Soren Kierkegaard.

For Kierkegaard, truth is "objective uncertainty," as he termed it, "held fast, in the most personal, passionate experience."[6] While the ironies of this statement abound, from pairing "objective" with "uncertainty," "held fast" with "uncertainty," and "objective" with "personal and passionate," the essence of the statement is stark. And what is the essence of such a mind-bending declaration? It is the cultivation of the capacity for awe.

The capacity for awe couples objectivity, or the effort to maximally apprehend, with uncertainty; it couples personal and passionate appreciation with the call to act on, decide about, or take a stand regarding that which one appreciates; and it couples ultimate faith (in what one decides) with doubt (and the ability to question as circumstances demand).

Appreciation, encounter, responsibility (or the ability to respond) and faith (against the background of doubt)—these are the earmarks of an awe-informed life, and for Kierkegaard, the best we humans can achieve.

AWE AS ADVENTURE, NOT MERELY BLISS

As can be seen above, awe brings an element of thrill—even anxiety— to the contemplative process. This is because awe, unlike the state of quiescent oneness, is suspenseful, unfinished. It is like the lamp-lit walk along a country road, or the bewildering gaze at a starlit sky; but it is also like the unraveling of a memory, or the anticipation of discovery on one's drive to work. Indeed, any experience can feel awe-filled because any experience can be tinged with the sense of adventure and risk.

Although we do not typically associate adventure and risk with contemplative or mystical states, there is no reason to deny that they can be compatible. Put another way, awe adds a Western element to contemplative and mystical forms of consciousness. To the degree that these forms can be seen as ever-unfolding, transitory journeys, they are eminently compatible with the adventurous sensibilities of awe. To the degree they are viewed as absolutes or ends in themselves, on the other hand, they are foreign to awe. Awe derives its intensity precisely from mystery. Whereas traditional Eastern or mystical perspectives emphasize the *harmony* of being; the sense of awe emphasizes the *mystery* of being.[7]

In short, awe is imbued with the sense of adventure or discovery. While awe does not preclude the more stereotypical elements associated with mystical states—such as a sense of oneness, serenity, and bliss—it generally does not "end" with them either. Instead it views them as transitory, glimpses along the many-faceted path.

3

THE AWE SURVEY: FORMAT AND BACKGROUND

In the spring of 2005, I began an investigation into the vicissitudes of awe with several remarkable people. All of these people were distinguished by their extraordinary stories of awe-based recovery in five general domains—education, drug addiction, chronic illness, depression, and aging.

Before exhibiting participants' stories, allow me to provide some background on my approach to studying them. Unlike many psychological investigations, I knew many of my study subjects with a modicum of intimacy. Most were my friends, and some were particularly close. This context, of course, has both advantages and disadvantages. The advantages are that I was able to achieve a degree of intimacy and rapport with participants that is rarely, if ever, achieved in more conventional research situations. On the basis of this intimacy, participants displayed a depth, candor, and subtlety of articulation that is, again, rarely achievable in more formal relationships and settings.

On the other hand, I cannot deny that my knowledge of my research participants may also have biased them. They may have been (and some of them assuredly were) influenced by my views from past conversations I had with them, or from writings of mine that I shared with them. However, I strongly feel (and I know participants would attest) that to whatever extent I have influenced them, they have all had strong predisposing sympathies with that influence. Further, they are all mature, highly developed individuals who, by the very nature of their interest in awe, have pronounced capacities both to question and discern.

Therefore, whatever shortcomings my approach may have had in regard to investigator influence, I believe they were more than made up for by the richness, intimacy, and range of participants' disclosures.

My basic format for this investigation consisted of a semi-structured interview, along with (in many cases) significant embellishments on that structure. For me, the structure provided a useful stimulus to guide and home in on key points of my inquiry. (Note that in a few cases, such as the reports of Donna Marshall, Julia van der Ryn and her students, Christina Robertson and her study participants, and comedian Jeff Schneider, I did not use the awe survey at all. On the other hand, I selected these pieces because they struck me as eminently relevant to the scope and testimonial aims of this book.)

The key points of my inquiry were: 1) How and why "awe" (as distinct from other or similar sensibilities) played a critical role in the healing or recovery of a major life challenge; and 2) to what extent was one's own awe-based recovery significant for the culture or society at large. To analyze these data, I used what roughly might be called a reflective analysis. Although this analysis was informal, it drew on the principles of reflective-phenomenological research design (see note 1 for this chapter).

Below I exhibit the aforementioned stimulus questions (see p. 23). I used this format for all participants excepting those noted, and applied it in both face-to-face interviews (as in the cases of Jim Hernandez and Michael Cooper) and through correspondence via e-mail (as in the cases of Fraser Pierson, Candice Hershman, E. Mark Stern, and Charles Gompertz). In all cases, I also conducted follow-up interviews to ensure the accuracy of the original reports.

One final point about this methodology: Much of my inspiration for this survey—and indeed, for this book—derives from William James's classic study *Varieties of Religious Experience* (1902). With his "radical empiricism," James opened the way for an intimate, subtly nuanced inquiry into the human condition, and it is to this essential framework that we now turn.[1]

Stimulus Questions for Interviewees*

(For possible publication in *Awakening to Awe*, written by Kirk Schneider)

(Note to interviewees: The below definition of awe is my own working definition. It is not intended to be final, but rather, a point of orientation. [Embellishment is welcome.] "Awe is a significant life-experience that combines the following holistic dimensions: the humility and wonder, thrill and anxiety of living; the capacity to be moved; and contact with the bigger picture of existence.")

1. What does the notion of awe mean to you?
2. What is the basis for your sense of awe?
3. What role has awe played in recovery or healing in your life (particularly with reference to a major life issue)?
4. What specific role has awe played in your specialty (e.g., as educator, therapist, etc.)?
5. What role do you see awe as playing in the larger scope of society?
6. How does awe contrast and compare with religion, psychotherapy, and other forms of recovery and healing in our society?
7. Is there anything else you would like to add about awe-based recovery or healing?

*Please try to be as thorough and yet specific and concrete as possible. The strong effort here is to reach and assist people who desire "recovery," but who are disillusioned or disenchanted with the prevailing remedies.

II

AWE-BASED AWAKENING: THE NEW TESTAMENTS TO SPIRIT

4

AWAKENING
IN EDUCATION

The stories that follow illustrate the power of awe-based awakening in an assortment of remarkable lives. Accompany me now as we discover this power firsthand, beginning with the pioneering testimonies of two educators: Jim Hernandez and Donna Marshall.

About fifteen years ago, Jim Hernandez, ex-gang leader, youth advocate, and spiritual firebrand, sought me out as a philosophical consultant—and we have been mutually consulting ever since.

Jim is one of the most multifaceted people with whom I've had the privilege to work (and in more recent years, to befriend). About twenty years ago, Jim's eleven-year-old son died of a rare and ravaging illness. About ten years before that, Jim had been a member of a Latino street gang and had seen many deaths, including the assassination of his younger brother. Out of the depths of his despair and search for a rejuvenated life, Jim began reading existential philosophy. Existential philosophy, which addresses renewal in the face of adversity, "spoke" to Jim in a way that no other worldview had, nor to this day, could.

Along with his reading, Jim began to explore alternative means to renew his life. Psychotherapy was a huge part of that exploration, but so was art (particularly that of Jim's ancestral Mayan culture), training as a counselor, and joining a healing community. At about the same time, Jim attended a local library to find material to supplement his training as a suicide prevention facilitator. As he glanced about the study area, his eyes came upon a book that fixed his gaze: *The Art of Counseling* by Rollo May.[1] Upon discovering this volume, Jim spent the rest of his time leafing through its illuminating passages. Soon thereafter, Jim was spurred by an impulse to call the author, who lived just a few miles away on a majestic seaside hill.

This call turned out to be a watershed event in Jim's life, for not only was Rollo May receptive to Jim's call, he also enjoined Jim to visit him at his home. This invitation was energizing for Jim and led to a touching exchange of gifts. Rollo, whom, as I previously indicated, I too had the privilege to befriend, gave Jim a signed copy of his *Art of Counseling*, and Jim, in turn, gave Rollo a ceremonial carving he had fashioned.

In the course of their conversation, Jim asked Rollo if he could study existential philosophy with him, and conveyed the significance of that perspective in his own life journey. While Rollo was sympathetic to Jim, he relayed that he was too old (approximately eighty at the time) and too limited to take on new students, but that he had a sense that I might be a viable alternative, and that Jim should give me a call.

And so Jim did, and for the next two and a half years, we embarked on a most rewarding and mutually enriching venture, reflecting on and experimenting with just how existential philosophy might support Jim's work. Over the course of this time, Jim began to draw on his counseling skills to work with some of the most hardened youth in his East Bay district of Concord, California.

In the ten years since Jim began his service as a youth violence specialist for the Concord Police Department, there has been not one violent death on his watch. Further, Jim has begun teaching a highly unique course in the Mt. Diablo school district, and this is where Jim and I, once again, converged on a common path. Based in part on the principles set forth in my book *Rediscovery of Awe*, and in part on his own special brew of spiritual, anthropological, and hard-won life experience, he proposed and developed an "awe-based" curriculum for fourth and sixth graders at Bel Air Elementary School, Mt. Diablo, California.

In September 2004, Jim and the vice principal of Bel Air Elementary, Donna Marshall, teamed up to support and find the funding for the "awe-based culture class" that we are about to discuss. This pioneering class, which has (as of this writing) lasted for the better part of two semesters and is expected to continue next year, has been presented on a voluntary basis during the aftercare period at Bel Air elementary. The class, according to Jim, was comprised fourth- and fifth-grade students from multicultural backgrounds, meeting once a week. The backgrounds included two Caucasian, one African American, one Vietnamese, and nine Hispanic students. The class was scheduled for twenty-four weeks and divided into four sections of six weeks. Each section covered a different aspect of a given culture: storytelling/writing, mask making, drumming and dance.

The concept of awe, Jim explained, "was introduced through artistic expression as students were encouraged to participate in the activities. The students were strongly encouraged (and given guidance) to be as creative as possible with imagination and creation of projects." To illustrate this sequence, Jim would introduce a theme, say, an indigenous Mexican carving, and tell a story about that carving. Then he would enjoin students to create their own story, music, and perhaps dramatic performance, based on the indigenous tale. Following these enactments, Jim would then lead a discussion period, inviting and encouraging students to not only reflect on their discoveries, but to consider the moral significance of those discoveries for their day-to-day lives.

Jim reported at the end of the second semester that "the program has been well received by administrators, teachers, and parents. . . . What has emerged as the foundation of the program," he elaborated, "is 'participation.'. . . The students in this class have created a safe haven, a community where they can express their creative selves, and feel safe while doing so. They have given their selves the 'freedom' to create [à la Rollo May's conception in his book *The Courage to Create*[2]]. As a result of their ongoing participation," he continues, "I have witnessed an increase in self-esteem and friendship which has made a big contribution to their resiliency."

On a balmy Friday afternoon in May 2005, I visited Jim at his school environs. I spent a full and energizing day observing Jim's awe-based culture class, participating in a question and answer period with the students, witnessing a student-created play and musical, and speaking in depth about the class with Jim, a parent of a student in the class, and the vice principal of the school, Donna Marshall.

What follows is my interview with Jim about his experience incorporating awe—not only in his elementary school class, but in his life, and with the youth he has so intensively served. Following this interview, I will then present my interview with Donna Marshall, who provides a close-up administrator's view of Jim's work.

One last point about Jim Hernandez: Several months before this writing, I nominated Jim to receive the 2005 Nobel Prize for Peace for his extraordinary work with the youth of the San Francisco Bay area. What I have come to realize since, in part from my experience at Bel Air Elementary, is that Jim is one of a cadre of remarkably dedicated professionals who are attempting to re-instill hope and aliveness in a generation of flagging souls, kids who crave discovery but who meet with admonishments, or who starve for affection, encounter, and guidance, but who enmesh with crassness, commercialism, and expediency. We have no higher task than to reach out to these devolving innocents, lest we, the innocents of our planetary future, devolve with them.

JIM HERNANDEZ: FROM GANG LEADER TO YOUTH EDUCATOR

KS: Jim, what is your notion of awe?
JH: My notion of awe is that it is a movement, a stirring of the soul. It's a stirring of the soul that is the bigger picture of all of us—which, as far as I can understand or experience it, is endless, limitless. And out of that soul, we experience . . . limited parts [which are shaped by] the dynamics and . . . physics of the world we live in.

If I take a look at the soul as the source of being (and nonbeing), I'm limited in looking at it. . . . [For example,] I can't fly like a bird. . . . The soul is like a big ball of clay and out of that ball of clay you can form a bird, and you can form a man, and they both have different dynamics once you put them into motion in this world.

And what stirs that soul, what's awesome, is that the person can look back at the ball of clay and say, wow, that's where I came from! That's my source. Wow, look what else came from that source [such as] a bird that flies . . . , a bat that flutters . . . , a newborn baby that I hear cry for the first time. It's the softness of a baby fawn. It's a bald eagle in flight that comes up with a trout in its talons. It's that awe that moves you. . . . It puts something in motion but it all returns back to that ball of clay eventually.

So my sense of awe is to have my soul stirred by my counterparts of that soul, in this limited space, in the temporal conscious existence, knowing that what really stirs me to my core are the things from the eternal core, the eternal sense. And when it moves me . . . then [I] know [I'm] alive. Then . . . [my] whole focus is not just on life in a temporal sense but LIFE, [as in] life is so grand, it's so wonderful.

KS: What role has awe played in healing and recovery in your life?
JH: When a person is in a place of despair it's very difficult for them to have their soul stirred, this [sense] of awe. So in recovery, what has been helpful to me . . . as I'm in the . . . process of [healing] is that stirring of the soul, that something phenomenal that happens. When I was in recovery—ACOA (Adult Children of Alcoholics)—for example, . . . [I was] able not just to chant the "serenity prayer" but to take it apart line for line. [The prayer goes as follows]: "God grant me the serenity to accept the things I cannot change, the courage to change the things I can, and the wisdom to know the difference." And that wisdom part is where the awe came for me. When things struck me at the core of my existence, I got the wisdom to be able to *discern* what I could change, and what I could not change [in terms of] what I was recovering from . . . and have the serenity to do that, to make those distinctions.

For me . . . what was good for my recovery was being in that place of despair, having my soul stirred. . . . [It] was probably like an endorphin release that [indicated] wow, I'm moved.

You get that serenity and you go from hopeless to helpless, and helpless is an entirely different place than hopelessness. If you're feeling helpless then the best way to get through that helplessness is to [appeal to] God to grant me the courage to change the things I can. . . . And once you get through the helplessness, then you can experience the awe, and that trust again.

And this is where [I] started to seek out people who had that wisdom, which led me to Rollo May, which led me to you, which led me to the authors and the books you see behind me living past and present.

Is [having my soul stirred] effective? Yeah, because what I was able to take from it in all my volunteer work, to working with gang members, to kids who were grieving from the loss of a parent, to the kids I work with today who have been bullied at school, is . . . to let them know that you can recover, you can recuperate, meaning bounce back from what has happened. That's how it's played an instrumental role in my life. . . . These [aforementioned] awesome experiences have helped me to bounce back.

KS: Can you say more about what you mean by God? Do you have a way to describe that source? I take it you're not talking about a conventional God . . .

JH: No, one of the dilemmas I ran into when I entered into ACOA is that [the group] constantly referred to their higher power, and . . . that you could turn your problems, your troubles over to whatever your higher power is, that you can "let go and let God," [meaning] that you can put trust in your higher power's corner. [But] that took me a while to do because when I came to that [gathering], I had given up on God in the conventional sense [given that I was] brought up Catholic, and all the difficulties I had, and the suffering, and all the losses I had. I realized I had no sense of what God is and no higher power. And I was uneasy with that realization.

But once I developed the higher power—and it was basically through reading a lot of Buddhism and Taoism that I adopted my higher power—the all-eternal . . . no-thingness. . . . Then where [the higher power] came from was not . . . proving myself to God or God proving himself to me, but [in my allowance for God to] "woo" me, move me, stir me, make me feel alive. And when that started to happen . . . I was finding myself being drawn to so many places in nature where that higher power moved me, [such as] climbing a mountain, or being in the desert or being in the snow; or sitting on a rock meditating and suddenly see this fox come by and pause. That's [when] I was reading "The Significance of the Pause" [from *Freedom and Destiny*] by Rollo May. And . . . [the fox] was pausing to make sure it's safe. And I realized I was in this longer pause than he was, and that he couldn't detect me. . . [But] the minute I would come out of that pause, he could, and would run the other way. By me relaxing and resting in that pause, I could enjoy his presence as long as I wanted, because he had no idea I was there; but yet I was there in the no-thingness of his no-thingness.

So that higher power has wooed me, has stirred me, but most important of all what it has done in a really awesome way is [the following]: When I was attending a conference on domestic violence [held by the Ernest Becker Foundation, in Seattle WA], one of the speakers did a talk on men who were abusive [toward their wives]. And she said what she noticed with these men is that none of them in their early years—and this is why she felt they were so abusive to their wives [in subsequent years]—had learned to self-soothe. And this is what the awe does for me; this is what the awe teaches me—how to pause and how to self-soothe along the way, so that there's less friction and conflict in my inner world.

It also helps [me and others] to be more fluid in this world. Now . . . most men today would see this self-soothing thing as sissyish or . . . girl stuff, [but] that's not self-soothing [as I mean it here] but nurturing in a different way. So the analogy here [in a way] that men can grasp is like this: Most men are really proud of their [automobile] engines . . . they can talk engines all day long;

how they take care of it, change the oil, make sure it has a long life, on and on. Well, we take a look at an engine and we talk about the friction and the heat that happens . . . you want to protect it from that friction and the heat. Now the self-soothing is . . . the internal oil coming up and lubricating the engine from the *inside* that cuts down on the wear and the friction from inside—there's an oil pump in there that delivers it to the bearings and the pistons and all throughout the engine; men can understand that, because without that [lubricating] the engine blows.

So the analogy I've been giving is that self-soothing is about that viscosity, that fluid and that "motor oil." And once I can get them to grasp that this is what you need to self-soothe . . . [then they] find they can be insulted, [they] can take a lot of stuff, [they] can deal with a lot of grief and not take it personally [because they] have that self-soothing going.

KS: So how would you describe that viscosity in terms of awe?
JH: Male socialization the way it still is in our society is that "boys don't cry," you don't discuss your problems, you don't show your feelings, you tough it up, you man it up, and you keep going. You get tough and you put the armor on—[yet] they wouldn't say the same thing about their engines. OK, you can rough it and tough it, that's a man, [but when it comes to the man's engine, if he doesn't] put any oil in it and doesn't change it [he would say,] "I can't do that."

Men have to understand—and women remind them of this all the time—that you can't do it the way you're doing it. You can't run this relationship, you can't run this life without this lubricant inside, which is again that fluid center that you talk about [in *Rediscovery of Awe*]. There's where that oil changing and replenishing comes from—it's that awe that stirs your soul, that keeps it moving, that keeps it going.

What this basically means is that we have to trust that this life is not a closed system—and we need to keep it going. . . . No matter what's going on, as long as that oil is pumping and reducing the friction, [one] can trust in that [like one can trust in a higher power].

KS: *How did you initially become stirred by awe?*
JH: I have, just like everyone else, the ability to be stirred and moved by outer experiences. What stirred me the most at an early age were two thought-provoking experiences. One was when I was a kid about 8 or 9 walking in Oakland with my mom [who] had some business to take care of, and there was this man laying in front of a doorstep with a newspaper covering him. It was a rainy, cold day, and I just stopped dead in my tracks. I just stopped. And I was looking at him and in my own mind [I said,] "doesn't anybody see what's going on here?" "How come this is happening, it doesn't make sense." "With all the world around him [and nobody helping]." My mom [then] explained to me that he's just a bum, and we walked away.

And that stirred me enough to say [inside], there's something wrong with this picture, that everybody walks by and ignores him. The entire world seemed to be in a denial that I was not willing to easily adopt. I acknowledged and recognized that another human being was suffering, and that bothered me.

Then the other thing that stirred my soul [was when I was in] middle school. [At the time] I went to church, to Catholic mass, like anybody else at the time, and like anybody else, I couldn't wait to go—"let's get it done, and let's get out of here." But then one day something stirred me enough [where] I actually saw the awe in the ceremony itself, something "talked" to me on another level to the point where I was suddenly moving to the point where I couldn't go back without becoming an altar boy, without becoming a part of that ceremony. And it was a big challenge because of the requirements the priests had set. I was the first to become an altar boy outside of a three-mile radius [which was generally precluded by the priest]. I made my appeal to Father Brennan and he gave me a chance and I succeeded in becoming an altar boy. So here was this middle school kid, taking seriously the role of dressing in robes, reciting the mass in Latin, the lighting of the candles, the burning of the incense, and the ringing of the bells . . . and the holy Eucharist, and being so—not solemn—but in awe, like "I'm part of this ceremony, this sacred ritual."

It became a natural, normal part of my life, this thing of ceremony . . . of sacredness, and though I don't follow that sacredness of the church . . . now I realize what I've been doing is searching for the ultimate, spiritual wave to ride. Currently I'm riding the waves of these ancient Mayan artifacts I collect and of Mayan lore and ritual. Years ago I rode the spiritual waves of the Catholic Church, today I'm riding the waves of the ancient shaman, and who knows the perfect waves I'll be drawn to ride on my spiritual surfboard next. And that's where awe continues to play an important role in my life, that at any given moment my soul can be stirred and that keeps me open to the wonder of life.

KS: What I'm resonating with here is that search part, that you keep alive in that search [where] new waves continue to evolve . . .
JM: Yes, and that the spiritual terrain is always changing in this world. . . . And maybe through the world and time there's these different shifts, different waves of spirituality and we follow them. . . . That's that awe, that wonderment.

KS: What role has awe played in your . . . violence prevention work and your work with the kids in the awe-based cultural curriculum?
JM: The role that's been played is to remind these kids, not so much to look away from their [destructive] behavior, as in denial . . . but to get them to look in another direction where suddenly they're awestruck by something. . . .

One kid I worked in particular with [is] Dan, and I have something here [Jim shows me] that Dan gave me, these Oriental chime balls. And one day he [gave me] these as a token of our friendship . . . because he knew I was a very spiritual person. [As context,] Dan was becoming a pretty hard-core gang member, and I took him out hiking in nature one day with a few of his other friends, and he just started goofing around acting silly, like a caveman—and he was awestruck at the whole place [Jim smiles]. And even his own friends [went into that] macho role and asked him, "What are you doing"? Again like those kids you saw today [while observing Jim's culture class], that natural resiliency came through; [the peer pressure] didn't stop him. He just answered them back: "When I get out in nature, I get WILD, I get CRAZY; I'm a NATURAL guy!" And they all started laughing

Storytelling (6 weekly sessions)	Students engage and learn through reading aloud folk tales from cultures around the world. Students write folk tales and read to class.
Mask Making (6 weekly sessions)	Students create masks in forms of characters from folk tales.
Drumming (6 weekly sessions)	Students learn to play various drum types and basic rhythms from cultures around the world.
Dancing (6 weekly sessions)	Students create dance movement to drum rhythms learned.
Final Performances	Students combine what they have learned and share with peers, parents, and the community through stage performances.

Figure 4.1. Jim Hernandez's Awe-Based Curriculum (eventually termed "Awe-Based Culture Class") for Fourth through Sixth Grade After-School Students at Bel Air Elementary School in Bay Point, California.

about it. Then they all broke that seriousness, because then they were being stirred. Then they were being moved.

So what I've been doing in my life is to not only share that experience with them, but the *potential* of it. Because while you're alive and you're still breathing, the potential still exists for awe to come your way and stir you and move you. It's so important to be open to that and be looking for it.

When I came into [the gang members'] lives, they saw where I was coming from, they knew that I'd been from the same place as they had been. And they . . . looked at that and went, "Not that he's OK and we can trust him, but how come he's OK after all he has been through?"

"And we know he's telling the truth." So I got their curiosity up, and pretty soon they were coming up asking me questions like, "How does this work? And what does that do? How did you get through all this?" And I shared with them how I got through it all, and so there was that trust there. And from there I was able to introduce to them, firsthand, how to put yourself in a position where, when awe comes, you can't miss it—how to put them directly in the path of awe.

I could also put them directly in the path of danger: "Stand here in the middle of the railroad track, you're going to get hit." [But what I urged instead was,] "Stand here in the middle of nature and sooner or later—because I've been here—awe's going to strike you. Something's going to move you out here, something will."

KJ: So inviting them into nature was very important.
JH: Yes, but there's an example also of something that got them to have experiences in *human* nature. When human nature comes along, just like regular nature, you can be over here and it can mow you down—just like a train—or you can be over here and it moves you. It uplifts you.

This one [teen] I worked with [was] Claudia, and we used to take the BART [train] together to the flea market. So I was always putting her through these existential exercises . . . about humanity and looking at people differently, and about not just trying to put yourself in their place but about scratch[ing] your head and [asking] to what degree is that [given] person in this crisis? What has gone on in their life, and where are they, depending on what's happened? So you could see somebody walking by [who] looked just fine, but you don't know that both of their parents just died yesterday in a car accident, but you wouldn't know unless they told you. [The point is] that everybody out there in society is at some level, in some of degree of anxiety or despair. So . . . I told Claudia here's the exercise we're going to do: "We're going to do the exercise ten times, and I'm going to start the first round. We're going to pick anyone out of the crowd and we're going to say something positive about them. So, for example, I picked that guy over there, he's got a nice jacket, he looks like a nice person. . . ." Then she goes, "Oh, you're wrong, Jim, I can't do this." She was so used to the negative. So [by the third round] she looked over at a police officer and she started snarling at him—automatically [putting him down]. And this was way before I worked for the police department. And then I say, "OK, on the next round we will select a person for each other to comment on," and she says, "Jim I know who you're going to pick," and I said, "You're right, it's the cop." And she says she can't do it; meanwhile, as we are watching him he stops at an area that was marked off with yellow tape to keep people from trampling the plants. The tape had been moved and he leans over and puts the tape back in place. As we are observing Claudia suddenly says, "OK, I like his assertiveness."

So finally, after a half hour, we got finished saying ten rounds of positive remarks . . . and she said, "Wow that took forever," and I said, so "OK, how long do you think it would take for you to make ten put-downs?" and she said, "Like that" [snapping her fingers]. "OK, there you are," I said, "that says something about our human nature, and today what I helped you to do was to embrace and have some different human experiences." Pretty soon, by the end, it was fun, she was moved by it, that awe came in. [And she was saying,] "Oh, look at this person, look at that person," and she was beginning to see people in an entirely new way.

And then we left the flea market and we were going down the street . . . and this homeless person came up to me and asked me for some money—and so I gave him five dollars. And [she asked me,] "What'd you do that for? He'll probably use it for drugs, alcohol, or something." And I said, "Yeah, but did you see what I did?" She goes, "No." Then she said, "Yeah, you gave him five dollars." But then I said, "Yeah, but did you see *everything* I did? Did you see the whole interaction?" She said, "Well I saw the money." And I said, "You saw the money and you got very angry . . . and you didn't pay attention to the rest." So I said, "This is what I did: He asked me for some money and I looked at him, and I said, 'Sure.' And when I took out the money . . . [and] handed it to him, I said, 'What's your name?' He said his name was Rick, and I said, 'Here Rick, I hope this helps you out, Rick.' And then he walked away."

She said, "I don't remember you saying his name." And I said, "You don't remember me saying his name? . . . You know why I said his name?" She goes, "No, why, what difference does his name make?" And I said, "That's just it—he's homeless, nobody even knows who he is. Do you know how good it feels to be addressed [with respect to] your name, as who you are?" She said, "Yes." [I continued,] "That's probably the first time he heard anybody [say his name] in months . . . years. Hearing his name was probably [the most important thing], the money was second after that."

So, the short of this story is that a couple weeks later, we were out on another [walk] . . . with some other kids who ordered a pizza and she said, "I'm going to go across the street, Jim, and get us some sodas." I said OK, and she came back and she looked so happy, so I said, "What's going on?" And she said, "I did it, Jim! I did it!" And I said, "What's that, Claudia?" And she was stirred, she was moved. And she said, "There was a homeless guy out there, he asked me for some change, [and] I asked him his name. And I said his name, and he got a smile on his face."

So that stirred her, that moved her [in keeping with my aspiration to] help students have nature move them, and at the same time, have human nature move them.

KS: Anything else about how you're bringing awe to the kids you're working with in the culture class?
JH: Yes, again [that which] I learned in my own ACOA recovery [regarding] the three rules of a dysfunctional environment —"you don't talk, you don't trust, and you don't feel," [is] that in a functional environment, you do talk, you do trust, and you do feel. And to feel that awe, to talk about it, and to trust it, that's . . . the spark of life that gives meaning to our everyday experiences.

And to bring this [realization] to the kids—to look at cultures, and past cultures, and to look at the symbolisms [of these cultures], masks and icons of some sort—what it basically does, is to [make it] safe to talk, if not about their own cultures, then about somebody else's. And usually they'll talk about somebody else's in a negative way, as a put-down [or] stereotype. [But] what's come out of this [class is] that it's moved kids in such a way that what they've experienced, and what they've learned about other cultures, and now their own, is far from the stereotypical view that people have.

And that opens them up, because then they're more open in their own recovery [in the sense] that they're building so much firsthand experience that they no longer have to recover [from that original experience]. They're having less experiences of the "don't talk, don't trust, don't feel." They're still having some of those experiences when they go home and out in the community. But having a place where that doesn't even come into play [is vital]. They open up, they spread their wings. . . . There's a different type of expansion that most people don't know about. It's sacred almost.

KS: So the awe is the inspiration and motivation to keep expanding . . .
JH: Yes, and it's also hope. That's something that as Viktor Frankl put it, is that hope for the future, that kept people going . . . [even] in the concentration camp. And I remember reading a passage out of [Frankl's book on the death camp—*Man's Search for Meaning*]. [It was] such a good passage about [his] experience of awe where he said we were all working and we all stopped and we saw the sunset. . . . And it was the beauty of the sunset that just moved us all [see Part IV of this volume for the quote], and it's like [they] were instantly lifted out of the hell of the concentration camp.

So, whether it's the kids I work with or the police officers, . . . you get to see firsthand that they all have the potential . . . to be stirred—in *any* moment, whether they have a uniform on, or whether they're a gang member or whether they're having a bad day as a student or as a parent or as a kid, [awe] can stir [them]. . . . That's the phenomenal part, that's what keeps me committed to my work and to sticking around to have such wonderful shared experiences with the students.

KS: You seem like the holder of the stirring, ever-ready to make that available . . .
JH: Yes, because I do that in my own life. I sometimes wake up and the stone [a ceremonial carving stone he has in his living quarters] will stir me . . . *or* [I find myself] headed to one of the remote areas of nature that I like. It just pulls me, it calls to me, and I'm gone, just getting up in the morning, getting in the car, and driving away.

KS: I should say something about this amazing place [that you live in] because it's filled with objects that radiate and that call to and remind one of the spectacle of being and the desire for adventure. [Jim has innumerable ceremonial stones, carvings, and shamanic objects in his living space, and it is a veritable museum of awe-based symbolism.]

JH: Definitely. And each one of these objects that you see, move me. . . . I go back to Aldous Huxley's book, *The Doors of Perception*, when he was on mescaline and commented he was "back in a world where everything shone with the Inner Light, and was infinite in its own significance." And so I can go to that room [in my home] to the things that shine from within, and go through those doors of perception. Meaning I can light all the candles that I have in there and [witness] all the crystals and paintings that start shining also from the outside when a certain light hits them . . .

KS: Like a prism?

JH: Yes, almost like a prism.

KS: So to concretize this a bit more with the kids, you are continually bringing in stories, sacred objects, drawing sacred symbols from various cultures, to spark their wonder, and also their connection to these stimuli in terms of their own lives? And then inviting them to create their own stories, their own adventure, with these objects?

JH: Yeah, and to also see that especially with nature there's an abundance of media to use. You've seen some of the rocks and stones [we used in class]—there's this abundance of different formats to play with. There are these little flat sandstones on this altar that I have that have been tumbled for thousands of years in riverbeds, and they become little flat disks almost. And years ago when my daughters were having this Brownie [Scout] convention [near] Half Moon Bay, I was just getting back from one of my vision quests in the mountains, I was really tired, and I joined up with them. . . . And here's this creek, so I went to lay down . . . and just crash for awhile. [Then] I woke up and I noticed those little stones in the creek. I picked one up and I whipped out this carving knife I had and just started carving a design in it. Next thing you know, I was just carving all these little intricate designs in the stones because it was so easy to carve. And I was very friendly with children, and this was even before my work with kids, and I look up and I hear all these kids [perched above the river bank] . . . and I . . . said, "Can I help you?" And they said, "Yeah, look at you Mr. Homeless," and these were just Girl Scouts. And I asked, "Is this any way for you to be acting out?" And they said, "What are *you* doing here?" [in a mocking tone]. And I could see what this [was about]: They're looking way down at this guy in a creek, a guy picking up rocks, who looked like whatever, so "let's pick on this guy."

So this whole group was on me and I said, "You know, I don't think you would appreciate it very much if I went and talked to your group leader." And they said, "What do you know about group leaders?" And I said, "Well, I'm here because my daughter's in the group here, I'm a parent here." . . . So finally they ran off, they stood up and got scared. . . . Then the next thing I had to wonder [about was how people would look at this] crazy guy in the creek scaring all the kids, so I left the creek and made my way back and joined up with my daughters. Later that night, when they were all [gathered] for the big campfire, the kids from the creek saw me. And they [said], "So you really are a parent." And I said, "Yeah." And it was like all of a sudden they were starting to apologize, so I accepted their apologies and I said, "Do you want to know what I was really doing down there [in the creek]?" And they said, "Yeah." So I showed them the stones . . . and they all went, "*Ah.*" They were looking at the designs and they said, "Oh, that's neat, can I have one of these?" And I said, "No, I'm going to give them to my daughters."

And so, this is kind of the effect I want the stories, artifacts, and artwork that I bring [in the class] to have on the students . . . that "oh, wow." I do a lot of drawing with them, and I have awestruck a couple of kids—not that I'm bragging—but I know the "in," it's personalizing [them], like you say. I walk into this elementary school classroom . . . thrust in by the principal, on a rainy day recess period, and I'm going OK, the students aren't sure of who I am or why I'm there and are looking at me with suspicion. . . . So I wait for the first one to approach who's kind of friendly, and I say, "Hi, my name is Jim, so, by the way, what's your name?" Then I'd get a piece of paper and draw their names in bubble letters, and I'd draw—which is popular today—. . . these little figures with flames around them [similar] to my artistic work, and they'd be like, "Whoa! He did it so fast!"

So when I personalize it, . . . [put] everybody's names in these bubble letters, pretty soon they're crowding [around me]—I'm getting to know them on a first-name basis, by doing the artwork, and then I hand it to them and it's a coloring page [where] they can fill [in the bubbles] with markers.

And this has been my entrance to many groups of young people . . . and all of a sudden they're looking forward to me coming next week because I'm going to finish the names. I ran out of time. And [they ask,] "Can you draw my mother's name, can you draw one for my friend?" And I'd say, "Sure." And so it's this whole medium again of art, itself, that [makes] them awestruck, [feeling,] "Wow, he can do this so easily, he's an artist."

I had this one kid who approached me in school today . . . this little second grader . . . and he was showing me this SpongeBob SquarePants character that he drew. And I was like, "OK, I like SpongeBob." But here's this second grader, Kirk, and these pieces of paper, where he had taken SpongeBob, and he made these scenarios with SpongeBob about to bungee jump and he put the expressions on his face and everything. He did another one that was a Santa Claus, and I said, "Did you really draw these? Do you realize these are really *good?*" . . . He just looked at me with a blank expression, then said, "Yeah, I know it's good; I had a great art teacher; you taught me how to draw in your after-school art class." . . . I'm like, "Damn, this kid's caught on fast. His inner artist was stirred and is now fast at work."

So, I was so moved, I went and bought [this kid] a sketchbook and colored pencils and I gave them to him as a gift. And I said, "Here, go with it, go with it." And that's that awesome thing where a lot of times when kids actually do draw, they look at the paper, see what they have drawn and . . . amaze themselves. . . . It's like looking at their own souls. It's like looking in the mirror. . . . We're conditioned

AWAKENING IN EDUCATION

not to look in the mirror and go, "Wow," because [you might be con-sidered] conceited . . . or egotistical. . . . But the whole awe thing is not about vanity, like, "I'm moved and look what I did." It's not vain, it's this whole intrinsic thing of "Wow, I'm alive, I'm here; I was just stirred, that shows that I'm here."

To me, that is one of the most rewarding experiences that I have [deriving] from the work that I do—when I see that suddenly hap-pen to these kids. And I get the awe in viewing it.

KS: So it seems you're giving permission to these kids . . . to open up.
JH: Yes, and that goes back to that [theme of] field work. . . . There are certain things that are permissible in [a field]. [For example,] in the field of your [therapy] office, people are given permission, and a lot of times they'll use it to open up, express themselves, speak from it. You go to a baseball game . . . and you have permission to play as strong and hard [as you can] on a professional level. You go to my classes . . . there's permission there, written and unwritten, that it's OK for expression.

KS: [And you] have so much to do with the permission. . . . You exude permission.
JH: Yeah, and . . . the awe is not just a random experience as much as it is a response to randomness. It can be . . . at times. [For example,] I get caught in a lightning storm and I go, "Aw, this is not going to happen very often, so I'm going to enjoy nature and its fury." I'll find a safe place under an oak tree and permit myself to be in the mo-ment. Whereas other people are running and cringing from it and don't want to be hit by lightning—they're afraid of that awe.

But with the kids especially, the awe is a cue. It's a cue for other things. Once the awe happens . . . it's a cue to express, open, speak, sing, laugh. Other people see the cue [and respond]. [In the] limited view of Isaiah [from the Bible], who saw God and cringed . . . it was this whole awesome, terrifying thing. And that was because in that moment, he didn't take the cue [to] relax and enjoy the moment of the here and now in the presence of God; and because he didn't know how to take that cue . . . the experience was horrifying. He saw all this [God's grandeur] and couldn't move with it. So those kids who you saw today [in my class] see these cues—some directly given and some nonverbally—and they move with them . . . they open up.

And one of the cues that worked in that class [was] the students hearing the girls on the violins and the clarinet warming up, they knew then what to do. That's why, if you noticed, I announced to the girls first, "Music section go ahead and warm up," [because] I knew that . . . once they took my cue, it would just ripple out on its own, automatically, . . . [and for the rest of them] it would be, "OK, here we go." And in a short period of time the group came together and performed their nature dance for us.

And the difficulty in society, and what we're all working against, unfortunately, is that [many] kids take these antisocial cues . . . [where] if somebody looks at them wrong, immediately, it's, "What are you looking at?" Or there's so many cues they take from listening to this rap music that's very negative . . . [like] "hate the cops or hate the parents" and all that. [The kids] don't realize that [hearing this music is] like reading cue cards.

[However] I point out to people in different ways, through metaphors and such, that it is possible in a pause to have a change [in] a course of action or in this case, reaction. . . . If you pause for even a half a second, there's a lot that you can do to change your course of action.

KS: Can you summarize your sense of what bringing awe to the kids can mean for society as a whole?
JH: Sure, the current path that the human race is on, of moving away from this awe . . . is [a place] where the kids are just getting cheated. They're not going to be able to experience the fullness of what we were exposed to on a natural basis as kids ourselves, forty something years ago. Here we are a half a century later, [and] they're told not to trust nature. . . . They're told that . . . if you go in nature you'll get poison ivy, poison oak; there's rattlesnakes, you'll fall and break your bones on these rocks and so on. . . . [They're told to] stay away from it—stay in this concretized world where it's safe . . .

So the bottom line here is that what we've done at the same time [in telling kids not to trust nature] is that we're also telling kids not to trust their human nature, 'cause it'll get you in a lot of trouble too. [On the other hand,] trust the technology of human nature.

So what I see with these kids is, where they're really going to have the opportunity to experience their own human nature is in this place of awe. And if they're shut down, and have the wrong cues, they're going to miss out on the moments of awe in their lives. And it's not like they don't have [this ability to experience their human nature] . . . but it's this loneliness or the feeling that something's missing in their life, and they don't know what it is.

KS: A longing?
JH: Yes, a longing, and what I've seen with these kids is that it's a deeper longing with each generation. Eventually, we're going to get kids . . . massing in self-sabotage or self-destruction, because I have witnessed this with a lot of kids. . . . That's the sad side, but the positive side is that it's not affecting all kids that way. . . . At any given time in our human experience, there are people who are constructing the world and people who are destructing and taking it apart. For example, you look at [U.S. President] Bush and the war machine, they're busy destructing . . . then there's other people like the Dalai Lama who are constructing a positive mind-set. I'm trying to get kids to a place where they are constructing a positive world view. [Although] there are groups throughout the world who are trying to do something to stop the destruction. . . . We're finding that it is very difficult if not dangerous to intervene. So I encourage our youth to construct, to build, to develop an inner strength so that if [other constructions, safety nets] are knocked down, there's still something in place within. . . . Let's move all the way to Taylorsville [a rural village in Northern California], [for example,] and let's create a community where awe is alive, a community like what you saw in my classroom.

We have those choices, we can move toward the awe and the construction/development of inner strength. What I'm excited about is . . . my next [project, which is] . . . to start to empower and work collectively with [some] existential [psychology] interns. . . . What I'm trying to do is to build an army of [these young interns] to get this awe-based approach into the school system. [And] if there's anywhere that I'd like to establish this approach, [it's] with the school psychologists. They, like me, are on the front line of assisting our youth with opening up to the awe, wonder, and splendor of life.

INTERVIEW WITH DONNA MARSHALL, VICE PRINCIPAL AT JIM'S SCHOOL

Following my interview with Jim, I had the privilege of speaking with Donna Marshall, the vice principal of Bel Air Elementary School of the Mt. Diablo School District. Donna is a bright and animated educator, with a refreshing passion for her vocation. I talked to Donna about Jim's class, her experience at the school, and about the need for awe-based education.

KS: Do you have any reflections about this class Jim Hernandez is teaching, bringing a sense of awe to the fourth graders and sixth graders?
DM: I've watched this class from the beginning. . . . When [it] was canceled [once] . . . the kids were devastated.

KS: Is that unusual?
DM: Very unusual.

KS: What makes this class unusual?
DM: That it's student-centered; that students are allowed to have conversations about what's important to them. They're allowed to have some ownership about what they're doing. They're not being told "today we are going to open this book up to this page," their ideas are very *valued*. Their thoughts are valued. When they come back [after a week], their reflection from [the previous] week is honored and valued. Whereas I think that today, teachers are so pushed to get all the standards in—in a hundred and eighty days—[that

they] don't have the time to listen to [students'] reflection about yesterday, [they've] moved on to today's lesson.

And it really is where education is now. So for kids to have this opportunity—they're loving it, this is what they want.

Realistically there's not enough time to get the state-mandated things done in the school year . . . so that discussion time, that thinking and talking, there simply isn't time for it. And it becomes a difficult decision that teachers have to make, and I think that most teachers are pushing on, and not allowing kids that talk time.

KS: What about this course is unique in regard to its focus?
DM: It's *very* unique in its focus. Bel Air is a Title One school which means our children are living in poverty, which means their test scores are low. We focus on reading and math at this school. Again, we don't have time for music. We don't have time for art. We don't have time for history—which in the big scheme, if a child can't read, they'll never be lifelong learners. So the goal to teach them to read is important, but a class [such as] Jim is teaching—about cultures, making the children feel valued because they have cultures; understanding cultures around the world, teaching empathy, and bringing in music—[is even more significant]. They are reading, they're doing more writing in that class than in a typical classroom, actually, and they *love* it. And they [consistently] come back.

There's no homework assigned, because it's not a required course; but these kids come back with writing every week. They've taken the time to write. Or if they haven't written [something] down on paper, you know they've been thinking about doing so because they come back ready to share their stories, their ideas.

KS: Is this [type of class] going on in any other school system?
DM: Not that I know of. . . . You need somebody educated enough to understand [creativity, cultural history, etc.], and there simply is not the money to pay somebody [who does]. We have about a hundred kids that are here everyday after 6 o'clock; it's a free day-care program. The people who lead those classes make barely above minimum wage—they are high school or right out of high school

students who don't have any understanding about sitting down and having a conversation with children. They play ball, and help them with their homework and do arts and crafts.

KS: [Do you mean] they don't have a contextual understanding about history and culture, etc.?
DM: Correct. Or even ability to really connect with kids in that way. You have to know when to lead them, when to give them information, and when to step back and let them process. And that's a very fine line, because if you let them process too long you can lose them, and they don't care [at that point].

I was able to find the money to pay someone—Jim—[who could manage that fine line and balance].

KS: Did Jim originally propose the course?
DM: It really was very mutual . . . and kind of came together. [Ironically], we started with a very concrete plan, "for example, in two weeks we'd do this and in two weeks we'd do that" . . . but we let it take on its own life.

KS: Was that in keeping with the philosophy of awe?
DM: Absolutely. So we had a structure back in September but we were both able to let that go, to let it go for where it needed to go.

KS: Have you noted any concrete behavioral effects on the kids, aside from what you've already mentioned?
DM: Yes. I noticed that the kids in that class are actually better problem solvers than they were at the beginning of the year. They're able to listen and work through things, and I don't think it's just their age—because I can compare that to kids their age, who haven't had that growth. I think their ability to feel heard and know that their thoughts are going to be valued [gave them the sense] that it's worthwhile to sit down and talk to me [when they had a given problem or concern. I think that] has been worthwhile. They're more able to say what went wrong, what should have happened, and what they're going to do next time—and *they're* able to come up with that [and not have to take their cue from me].

I think that giving kids the opportunity to talk, have conversation, gives them the ability to think. If you're just putting information into their heads, you don't have to think. And so they know this process is valued.

As I say, it's not the fault of teachers; it's just a difficult time to be in education right now. We need to have some change or we're going to end up with kids who are not thinking, thoughtful, creative human beings.

KS: One last question about the sense of awe–do you have any feel for what bringing that dimension into the schools could mean for these kids as they develop?
DM: I believe that bringing [awe] in is probably one of the most important things that we do. I think that bringing awe to children gives them the wonder which gives them the interest and the *want* to know. And you're never going to know if they're going to want to study cultures, or animals, but if they have the awe, that drives their interest. I think we're doing a huge damage to children by taking that away. And I understand that they have to learn to read, but teachers have to find the time [to bring in the sense of awe] or I think we're damaging the children.

And I see the effect [of that damage] every day, actually. I know the teachers who have no awe in their lives. Those are the [ones who have] students who are in my office on a regular basis. Now [those students] are smart enough to get out of class because they know they're going to have a conversation with me. Going to the [awe-informed] classes, I never see these children because they get everything they need from their teachers.

JULIA VAN DER RYN AND A CLASS IN AWE-INSPIRED ETHICS

In the spring of 2005, I was contacted by Julia van der Ryn, an instructor at Dominican University of California, in San Rafael (Marin County). Julia had just completed a semester teaching an undergraduate class in service-learning and ethics, and was excited to convey her findings about the impact of my previous book, *Re-discovery of Awe*, on her students. Service-learning is a teaching and learning method that integrates academic curriculum with meaningful service that meets community-identified needs and course learning objectives. It is an educational approach that can bridge the teaching/learning gap in moral philosophy between thinking well and acting well, or between theory and practice in any course. Service-learning also represents a paradigm shift that encourages awe in a variety of ways. As Julia says, "using service-learning and books that I was drawn to, I began, with my students, to see and experience the ways in which the personal meaning that each of us seeks is ultimately intertwined with our moral stance in the world. As philosopher John Dewey contends, moral growth does not happen in a vacuum; we grow and mature through interaction with our environment and other people." The basic thrust of the class is for students to learn about ethics by going out into the community and practicing/applying their ethical knowledge to real-life issues rather than hypothetical discussions. In this context, students examined their community work in the light of several readings, including *Rediscovery of Awe*.

Below is a sample of the students' testimony about the impact of awe on their lives and the lives of those they served. Not only does this testimony highlight the value of learning more about awe and awe-based services (e.g., supporting, tutoring, counseling), it also accents the value of incorporating awe into one's very experience of life. Consider the following commentaries, introduced by Julia.

Julia van der Ryn (JV): The following student worked in an after-school program at a middle school.

After finishing *Rediscovery of Awe*, I also have another goal for myself. I want to help enhance the students' educational experiences by chalking them full of awe. I am not exactly sure how I need to go about doing this, or how I can personally shift the after-school program to be more "awe-based," but I'm definitely thinking about it. One idea that I have is to have regular field trips to places around Marin County: hiking at Mount Tamalpais, visiting the Dominican University campus for a tour, going to an art gallery, etcetera. These are ideas that I will have to present to the coordinator of the program.

JV: Another student worked at a high school helping behind the scenes of their theater group. She spent time consoling one girl whose mother had recently died.
Having to console this girl was one of the hardest things for me to do. My life has been so very blessed . . . I was reminded of this experience as we were reading *Rediscovery of Awe* because Schneider spends an entire chapter discussing the significance of pain. One line he uses from S. A. Rubin's dissertation, "The Experience of Tragic Optimism," really struck me, "Because if everything's wonderful, it wouldn't even occur to you that it couldn't be" (p. 130). This brought me back to that day with the girl. Before that exchange I had somewhat forgotten about mortality and had taken [life] for granted. . . . But now that I have that realization that life will not always stay wonderful, I have a greater appreciation for [it]. . . . Also, it is my calling as someone who is lucky to help those who may not be as lucky, to cope with and embrace the fact that their life will be a new and different type of wonderful again in the future.

JV: The next student worked with retired —very elderly—Dominican Sisters.
I have accepted the fact that life is not meant to be bereft of hardship. As Schneider stated in *Rediscovery of Awe*, "We must recognize that the capacity to tolerate . . . strife is one of the hallmarks of maturation and that without such a reserve, there is almost no chance to thrive" (p. 40). [In light of this], not only have my fears been dispelled, I have also gained a newfound understanding about life: it is meant to be great as well as terrible. Specifically, what Schneider said about struggle in life now makes sense. . . . One must undergo hardship and pain to be able to live a life of awe. Working with the sisters has illustrated this point.

The following year, Julia sent me these equally poignant testimonies.

JV: Stephane is an adult student who was a teen mother herself. She chose to work tutoring pregnant teens who were trying to pass the exit exam. After the first day there she didn't want to return because all her old feeling of inadequacy rose to the surface. But she kept at it and, I think, had a real breakthrough. She wrote:

In *Rediscovery of Awe*, Schneider talks about creating a fluid center in personality and development. He said "the fluid center begins and unfolds through awe, the humility and wonder of living" (p. 10). In going every week to spend time with these girls and in tutoring them in their schoolwork, I saw perhaps the first glimpses of awe unfolding as they contemplated the birth of their child. As it is with any expecting mother, no matter what age, the pending arrival of your first child [prompts] one to reflect upon the miracle of life. While this moment of awe may be short-lived for many of these girls due to the extenuating circumstances of their lives, I like to believe that a seed has been planted for them to reconnect with the place in their heart when they believed in the awe of life—their own, the community they live in, and the possibility to make some of their dreams come true.

JV: The next piece is from Colleen—a twenty-year-old politics major. She worked with Youth Court and with the Marin Aids Project [MAP]. I have included a few paragraphs because this is such a powerful statement.

In service we are forced to shift our life course from ego to egoless. As students, we are filled with ego, constantly striving to fulfill our duties as student, child, friend, employee, sibling, and the list goes on. We become less and less responsible as members of society and more members of a private club, one which is centered around one's self. We are instructed to do what is necessary for ourselves, for our future. We are taught that education is more important for future success in a capitalist society, than as a whole mind and body experience which should enlighten us and prepare us to be active members in society. We are taught to live life [in accord with] what our society dictates to us; money is power, help yourself instead of others, and the ego-filled mantras continue.

In service, we are allowed to break out of this realm. We are forced to do something which may not be typical to our nature or awareness, to do something that is not easy, and makes us look through a different lens. In service, our experiences are not always pleasant; they may be very difficult to view or accept. Service is our opportunity to surpass convention and to do something that will inspire awe. Through experiencing awe, we revert back to our natural selves. And although it may be difficult, sorrowful, or painful, it is through these negative experiences that one can truly find wonder. Schneider sees the cultural revolution that we as a society have undergone. Service is a way in which we can make a positive cultural revolution, one which will impact the greater whole.

My service opportunities have brought Schneider's themes to life. In my experience with Marin County Youth Court, I rediscovered awe. The children continuously gave me hope in the future and belief that there are children who are still being taught to care about world issues. It stills my heart whenever I walk in and hear them talking about current issues and debating them heatedly, speaking from their hearts. They look like children, but their personas in the capacity of political discussion are very mature.

In my work at MAP, I encountered different people from a variety of backgrounds and life experiences. Awe is inspired through their stories. Each has felt compelled and comfortable telling me about their private lives. While this is not condoned by MAP, for fear of breaking confidentiality, the clients are inclined to share their lives with me, and in doing so, I share a little of myself as well. This has reestablished the feeling of interconnectivity with society. For the most part, I just listen as they tell their stories reflecting on experiences in relation to my own. It is through this exchange that we both benefit in rediscovering a sense of wonder. We each come to realize that every person faces life's hardships and although mine do not come close to most of their stories, there is nonetheless a mutual success.

Finally, Julia sent the following longer reflections over the last year.

JV: A religion major begins and ends her final paper with the recognition of contradiction as integral to greater humanity.

The definition of ethics is both simple and complex; paradoxical and present in every moment. Becoming an ethical being can be an ambiguous struggle to obtain a self that lives a life worth leading, and helps others do the same; it is becoming "the self that is inspired by choice, imagination, and love" (*Rediscovery of Awe*, p. 45). Service-learning, in conjunction with applied ethics, can be a tool on the path to a lifestyle in which ethics, justice, and reflection are inherent aspects of everyday life. My experiences as a student tutor at County Community School, in combination with course texts and discussion, have contributed to my deeper understanding of good and evil, within the individual and society, as well as helped me develop reflective practices to maintain that understanding and encourage it in others. . . .

What seems to be the struggle of County Community School, and of activists and philosophers in society, is to maintain that balance between the feeling of insignificance of the oppressed and the luxury of magnificence that other tiers of society experience. As Schneider comments, "Few are willing to acknowledge both their smallness, humbleness before creation, as well as their boldness and capacity for adventure" (p. 51). This humility and boldness is inherently linked to the dichotomy of good and bad within the person and society. The simple, yet supremely difficult practice of maintaining this balance is involved in the cyclical act of self-reflection and holy, ethical action. People and society will continue to move forward; but where this forward movement takes us—whether it is better or worse than our current situation—is dependent on each human's ability to think within herself, realize her paradoxes, and work with others to maintain the balance.

JV: Another young woman writes about what she saw as the failure of the educational system for the students she tutored.

When I first started tutoring, the question that always seemed to creep up was "why"? Why take the time when you're busy? Why tutor a person who doesn't seem to care? Why help others? The

Golden Rule is nice in theory, but not so much in practice. . . . The immediate anxiety I felt as a tutor was whether or not I would connect with my student. . . . I have always had a desire to help people, ever since I wanted to be a doctor like my grandfather, but despite my good intentions there are few times that I have actually helped strangers. Wanting and doing are two completely different things in service. . . . I worked with several different students over the semester. I saw students who had their own problems outside of school, but still managed to be in class. I think the system of teaching is flawed. I found myself doing the same things I had hated in high school, focusing on getting the right answer but not thinking critically about the problem. When I worked with just facts and rules, I found it hard to connect with students. When I asked them about themselves, it was entirely different. In order to help another person, there needs to be some level of connection.

Kirk Schneider writes that the problem with education today is that it "fetishizes." "Fetishization is the narrowing down and confinement of thoughts, feelings, and sensations" (*Rediscovery of Awe*, p. 88). We are training the future generations to give answers and not necessarily opinions. We are confining the learning process, crippling imagination, and stamping out radicals. Education should be knowledge and wisdom passing from one individual to another. It should not be about letter grades and test scores, but those are the things that show up on paper. A girl I tutored one day didn't talk to me for a full ten minutes. I found that she was struggling with both the English language and being shy around strangers. You have to be able to see beyond surface issues into what's really affecting another individual. Service, for me, is seeing the side of a person that is not immediately visible. Quality of education, unfortunately, is measured by numbers, not by positive experiences.

This system is failing, and the students I worked with were some of the first victims of the bureaucratic nightmare known as public education. If teachers are forced to focus on creating automatons, then we are systematically creating disconnection in our society. We are becoming numb, lost in fixing what isn't broken and ignoring what's in pain. We want everything to be solved at the speed of light and yet maintain attachment to nothing. Schneider writes: "I am concerned about the increasing casualness of society —the quick fix and throw away mentality. If you're feeling blue, pop a pill; if you disdain where you're living, go somewhere else; if you don't like your family tradition, adopt a new one; if you don't like what the government is doing, lose yourself on the Internet; if you're dissatisfied with live encounters, indulge in 'chat rooms.' If you don't like Western (or Eastern) values, make up your own, etc. Where are we going with all this haste . . . ?" (p. 7). The same goes for solving social issues. The mentality that if we throw enough money at the problem it will go away does not work. While education is in desperate need of funds, it also needs respect. Teaching, while considered a noble profession, is not necessarily an economically viable choice for college graduates. If you teach, you're probably not doing it for the money. But there are still two different kinds of teachers, effective and ineffective.

JV: Finally, a returning student in her sixties (who is now also in a graduate program focused on healing) writes.
Jeffrey is a teenager I recently tutored at Canal Alliance who helped me witness my evolving being. As we worked together on his homework assignment, Jeffrey also taught me about awe. "The first principle of awe is appreciation" (*Rediscovery of Awe,* p. 8), explains Schneider. The author further clarifies, "Appreciation is immersion, the setting aside of time, for that which is investigated. To appreciate an anxious individual, for example, I must stay with him for a concerted period. I must open my senses to him. . . . I must also open my feelings, imaginings, and intuitions to that person" (p. 8).

I observed that Jeffrey was anxious as I inquired about his homework. He told me in a low, mumbled voice that he was doing fine, and did not need any assistance. I could have found another teenager to help, but my intuition, imaginings, and feelings told me to stay with Jeffrey. As I opened my senses to this anxious individual, we both had an opportunity to experience awe.

This experience of awe came in the form of appreciation. Because I asked Jeffrey if he would be willing to help me understand what his teacher expected, he consented to let me look over a question-naire he was attempting (unsuccessfully) to fill out. The answers were related to a story in English which he was expected to read and comprehend. I looked over the eight-page copy of the story, and noticed some very difficult English words and was curious about Jeffrey's comprehension. So I asked him about the Spanish transla-tion of some of these words, and told Jeffrey I needed help with my Spanish—which is true. But my main motivation was to pronounce these English words aloud so he could hear the correct English pro-nunciation. I then asked Jeffrey if he would like to read the story aloud in English, and he said yes.

I affirmed his reading ability and we laughed and discussed some of the silly passages of the story, and when it came time to return to the questionnaire, he was now eager to answer the questions. I ob-served his anxiety disappear as he sat taller in his chair with a smile on his face and a gleam in his eye. I imagined Jeffrey was filled with wonder and awe that he had mastered a difficult assignment, and that he would carry that feeling of accomplishment with him into school the next day.

I also walked away from Canal Alliance that day feeling taller. I felt humbled that I had been given the gift of awe—to witness Jeffrey's mastery of a difficult assignment. I also marveled that these teenagers, who speak very little English, are expected to learn and complete difficult homework. I appreciate how complicated these assignments can be without a tutor. Even so, I perceive that Jeffrey and I had a mutual appreciation of our time together. I am proud I opened my senses to Jeffrey, and I am indebted to service-learning for giving me this experience.

5

AWAKENING FROM
CHILDHOOD TRAUMA

Childhood trauma is a tear in the veneer of stability. What was once familiar, mapped out, and routine is now deranged, shattered, and askew. What was once a reliable greeting or movement is now a vacancy, perversity, or threat. Yet what is left by this apparent quagmire is all-important, for, like so much in life, it is two-edged. On the one hand, it can scald and cause lasting damage; on the other hand, it can inform and foster enduring renewal. While it is not always clear what will promote these contrasting effects, the sense of awe, or the realization of life's majestic scope, appears to align with the renewal side of the continuum. In the stories to follow, J. Fraser Pierson and Candice Hershman both awaken to awe in their own respective ways: Pierson in her attunement to nature and the treasures of the sea, and Hershman through more local and internal modes. Whichever their paths, however, they each model an approach to brokenness that infuses life with grandeur—and the humility, likewise, to profoundly appreciate it.

J. FRASER PIERSON AND THE AWE OF NATURAL LIVING

J. Fraser Pierson is an extraordinary soul. As a witness to her father's descent into madness, she has boldly gathered the means to avert her own downward spiral, and to find her way to awe. Fraser, as her friends call her, is both a professor and a sailor. She is a psychologist and a naturalist, and a loving, thoughtful colleague. I met Fraser through our mutual mentor, James Bugental, with whom we coedited *The Handbook of Humanistic Psychology*, and I have cherished our connection ever since. Fraser sails for weeks and sometimes months with her partner-husband, Jeff, but little did I know, until undertaking this book, of the stormy seas she has navigated over the course of her lifetime, and of the lessons she has absorbed, which she will now impart.

KS: What does the notion of awe mean to you?
FP: Awe is an exhilarating, multidimensional phenomenon: it is a portal to transcendent consciousness. Moments of awe punctuate my life with exclamation marks of wonder, mystery, reverence, and grace. Awe is inspired by a marvelous event or the extraordinary in the ordinary (e.g., a pod of exuberant humpback whales engaged in collaborative bubble-net fishing; eye contact with a wild orca surfacing from the inky-blue depths; my dog's paw resting in my hand, our heartbeats in sync; the setting quarter moon melting like butter into the sea during a midsummer, offshore sail). Awe's afterglow illuminates my worldview; its warmth fuels feelings of abundance, generosity, and love toward all beings. Occasionally, my experience of awe is suffused with anxiety or fear. These feelings are associated with bearing witness or being subject to powerful forces that pose a threat to existence or are beyond my ken and control (e.g., the intense energy of an earthquake, hurricane, flood, or extreme psychological disturbance). As Emerson observed, "Nature is not always tricked in holiday attire."[1] My story of awe and healing spans the spectrum.

I find events that evoke awe are utterly absorbing, physically riveting, and profoundly, emotionally arousing; they are in essence, soul stirring, both in the moment and in their wake. Awe shakes me out of an every day, "taking life for granted" frame of mind into which I unintentionally slip. Awe brings me fully into the present moment. It is a vehicle, which transports me to a wilder, unconditioned self, vibrantly in touch with *being* (as opposed to doing), calling, passion, and the divinity in all forms of life, the mystical and the sacred.

Tantalizing yet fleeting, hints of enlightenment often accompany awe. In these moments, I feel a shift in *knowing*; it is as if I have suddenly awakened, with perception expanded and heart lights ablaze. I think to myself, "What a wonderful world!"

Try as I might, the full-bodied richness of awe eludes cerebral definition; it simply bursts the seams of intellectualization. I believe notions of awe are more vividly shared through narrative, or better yet, poetry, art, theater, and dance, the mediums that promote heart-to-heart connections and vibration between souls.

I experience awe in a variety of circumstances, particularly when the extraordinary or the ineffable is encountered but also in more commonplace moments when my senses, mind, and heart are receptive. The latter seems to be the key. For example, when a red-tailed hawk glides upon the thermal air currents just above my truck on a country road and I catch a glimpse of her glorious burnt sienna feathers backlit by sunlight like cathedral glass, I am flooded with awe. Adrenaline surges through my body; my pulse quickens; my breath catches, and then deepens; and my spirit soars with the vision.

Similarly, I experience a surge of awe when surprised by the exuberant, acrobatic maneuvers of Pacific white-sided dolphins surfing the wave created by our sailboat's bow. Dolphin visits are enchanting, particularly at night when they stir the phosphorescent organisms in the water, sending diamond sparkles whirling away into the wind and wake. The dolphins arrive out of the depths or across an expanse of ocean seemingly for the sole purpose of interacting with *Storm Petrel*, our sailboat, and perhaps, with us onboard. Alone at the helm on midnight watch, under a canopy of stars, I like to think that it is both curiosity and desire to engage that draws these sociable animals to our vessel. I am amazed and thrilled by such encounters in their environment and on their terms.

Dolphin visits leave me in an exhilarated, yet contemplative mood. Henry Beston's poignant philosophical reflections in his remarkable book, *The Outermost House,* express what evokes my feelings of awe during these star-spangled moments. He wrote,

> We need another and a wiser and perhaps a more mystical concept of animals. Remote from universal nature, and living by complicated artifice, man in civilization surveys the creature through the glass of his knowledge and sees thereby a feather magnified and the whole image in distortion. . . . For the animal shall not be measured by man. In a world older and more complete than ours they move finished and complete, gifted with extensions of the senses we have lost or never attained, living by voices we shall never hear. . . . They are not brethren, they are not underlings; they are other nations, caught with ourselves in the net of life and time, fellow prisoners of the splendor and travail of the earth.[2]

That the wild dolphins, fellow sentient beings, occasionally choose to meet me at the interface of our environments is wondrous. We acknowledge one another's presence as we dance in harmony to the cadence of the swells. I muse that we splendidly serve our respective nations as ambassadors; the extraordinary gift of their visits profoundly moves me.

I have also discovered that the *extra*ordinary is all around us if we know how to perceive it. My dear mentor and friend, the late psychologist James F. T. Bugental (1915–2008), marvelously demonstrated this outlook when I visited him in the hospital as he recovered from hip surgery several years ago. At one point in our visit, he gazed out of the large window of his first-floor room and tenderly spoke of the beautiful ballet performed by the trees outside to the steady tempo of the summer breeze. "Look at the ballerinas," he said with wonder and reverence. We sat in silence for a few moments enthralled by the spectacle. I enjoyed Jim's capacity for perceiving the world through awe-colored lenses (as did kindred spirits, Emerson and Whitman), even in the midst of painful circumstances. For over five decades, he consistently modeled such an inclusive vision of the world through his contributions as a pioneering psychotherapist, author,[3] teacher, and leader of intensive workshops on the art of the existential-humanistic approach to psychotherapy he developed.[4]

Another illustration of perceiving the extraordinary all around us is drawn from observations while researching the adaptation and socialization of Colossus (his "stage" name), a western lowland gorilla transferred from a traditional zoo environment to one that offered a more enriched habitat.[5] I had the privilege of getting to know this magnificent silverback, at least as much as possible in a human controlled environment, over a period of several months while he resided at The Zoo, in Gulf Breeze, Florida. Often as I stood around the perimeter of his compound recording his behavior in thirty-second intervals, fascinated by every nuance of expression, I overheard the conversations of the human primates in the vicinity. If Colossus was sleeping or sitting quietly, it was typical to hear something like, "He's not doing anything" or "Let's come back later when he's more active." Such comments occurred after watching Colossus for a minute, at most. Hurried, senses impaired by expectations of entertainment, these visitors missed the opportunity to fully perceive and appreciate Colossus in all of his glorious "gorilla-ness." He was an amazing being. I experience a fresh tingle of awe each time I look at my favorite photograph of Colossus propped on the bookshelf in my office. He is looking directly into my eyes with a soft, relaxed expression on his face. Mutually held direct gazes are unusual between a silverback and another adult gorilla, and I had been mindful of this in my interactions with him, always deferentially averting my gaze in respect. This photograph shows a cherished, elegant exchange of trust and intimacy in primate-to-primate nonverbal language.

I believe experiences of awe can be optimized and that receptivity is correlated with a celebratory attitude toward life and Nature (capitalized, as was the custom among nineteenth-century American Transcendentalists). As Ralph Waldo Emerson wrote in *Nature*, his first book, "The stars awaken a certain reverence, because although always present, they are always inaccessible; but all natural objects make a kindred impression, when the mind is open to their influence."[6] I am more likely to experience awe if my perceptual faculties (i.e., the capacity to clearly see, hear, touch, taste, and feel that which is in my environment) are unfettered by fatigue, distraction, or the kind of socialization that reinforces "fitting in," as compared to being authentic and trusting the compass of my unique experience.

Nature provides a wellspring of awe and ignites an ever-intriguing quest to know the Source. The feeling is reminiscent of admiring a painting or sculpture. I like getting to know the artist. Awesome events of the kind highlighted are cherished gifts from my Creator and serve to vividly affirm my interrelationship with Life in its amazing, myriad forms. Awe nourishes and "restores my soul,"[7] and infuses me with courage, so that I may more heartily embrace Life—its joys *and* vicissitudes, and in so doing, offer my unique contributions to the world.

KS: What is the basis for your sense of awe?
FP: The capacity for awe comes with the terrain of being a person and is quite possibly present for all sentient creatures. (I am certain of this shared capacity when I observe my golden retriever sitting motionless at the water's edge gazing out to sea, lavishly cloaked in the fiery red, deep plum, and gold infused light of a Pacific sunset.)

I am particularly receptive to our birthright when in the natural world, immersed in favorite activities such as hiking, sailing, and beachcombing or when deeply engaged in relationships characterized by the openness described by philosopher Martin Buber.[8] Profound psychological resonance or attunement with another is the hallmark of such openness. In times of turmoil or stress, I recover my center by drawing upon the treasured experiences of awe I hold within my heart or consciously and fully savor the beauty in my immediate vicinity.

Awe has illuminated my life for as long as I can remember. I grew up in south Florida at a time when there were still plenty of fireflies to chase on summer evenings; multitudes of giant blue crabs scrabbling across the low lying roadways during early summer migration; mangrove trees with twisted roots to climb when searching for prehistoric-looking horseshoe crabs or pretty shells in the warm, shallow waters of Matheson Hammock; the occasional hairy tarantula stowaway among the sweet bananas imported from Jamaica; wooded areas with dense palmetto bushes that formed mysterious green, leafy caves to explore; ubiquitous, luscious red, pink, and yellow hibiscus flowers; majestic, thick branched banyan trees to climb and to serve as pirate ships or other manifestations of my imagination; and clean stretches of white sand beaches that showcased magnificent sparkling Atlantic sunrises and sizzling Florida Bay sunsets. Invitations to awe were everywhere.

My parents and Scottish maternal grandparents (a union of "highlander" and "lowlander") fanned my youthful sense of wonder and curiosity. I enjoyed the privilege of growing up within a loving, well-educated family that instilled an optimistic self- and world-view, a secure base from which to respond to the challenges of life and to explore its mysteries. Travel introduced me to the diversity of customs, lifestyles, and opportunities across North America, as well as to the astounding biodiversity. The sensuality of place[9] captivated my imagination and quickened my spirit then as it does now.

Love, mystery, and the miraculous permeated the biblical stories and stimulating sermons of the liberal United Presbyterian church in which I first began to acquire my spiritual bearings. Interestingly, I have recently learned through searching historical records dating back to 1630 that a number of my paternal ancestors were influential members of the clergy, which adds to my speculation (with a flutter of awe) that awareness and appreciation of the numinous may be "in my bones." I also believe that I am naturally inclined toward experiences of awe through the contributions of my Celtic heritage, which is rich in mysticism and romanticism, and values both sensual and intuitive perception. The "ripplings"[10] of my ancestors seem to reverberate in my worldview. My immediate family members distinctly influenced my receptivity to awe.

My mother and Celtic grandparents, with whom we lived after my parents divorced, modeled deep and vibrant spiritual beliefs that simultaneously drew upon and exceeded the boundaries of Presbyterian doctrine. For example, my grandfather, an intellectual and spiritual voyager, entertained the revolutionary ideas expressed by the renowned teacher Jiddu Krishnamurti and notions of a cosmic consciousness. He also studied the contributions of the classical Greek philosophers and those of major nineteenth- and twentieth-century Western philosophers. He was active in his church and community but not intellectually restrained by convention. The implicit message permeating our home was that life is a grand quest that requires a sense of adventure, loving interdependence, and the courage to continuously seek deeper, personal answers to questions concerning existence. Faith and searching were viewed as mutually compatible.

My capacity to wonder was also encouraged in other ways. Most nights while [I was] in elementary school, Mom read classic fairy tales from around the world to my brothers and me. These bedtime stories were not for the faint of heart. The heroines and heroes were always noble, brave, and clever, of course, but they were also complex individuals who gained insight, compassion, and soul through over-coming challenges and finding their ways through perilous, shadow-filled woods. The characters engaged with the mysteries of life, they "enter[ed] the forest at the darkest point, where there [was] no path,"[11] which often included confronting dragons, trolls, and witches, and eventually triumphing over the trials these creatures presented. Awe, as a spur to courage (or heart), permeated the tales as it did in the vivid yarns my father created before he was irrevocably possessed by symp-toms of schizophrenia. His imaginative version of Herman Melville's *Moby Dick* romantically personified the character of the white whale; he became a "superhero" of mythic proportions far beyond Melville's portrayal. My father was a good storyteller and his exciting, awe-inspir-ing tales of this remarkable cetacean remain a bright legacy.

KS: What role has awe played in recovery or healing in your life?
FP: John Muir's eloquent reflections come to mind as I consider my response to this question.

> Everybody needs beauty as well as bread, places to play in and pray in, where Nature may heal and cheer and give strength to body and soul.[12]

> I am well again, I came to life in the cool winds and crystal waters of the mountains.[13]

Awe has played an integral role in healing the rent in my heart and in my family system rendered by my father's gradual fragmentation into full-blown, unrelenting schizophrenia, symptoms of which were often a shocking departure from our previously shared reality. Awe-based inspiration served as a powerful counterbalance, even an antidote, to the confusion, anxiety, and sadness swirling around and within me.

I sometimes think of my father as dying twice. The first time was a slow, increasingly painful demise that eventually eroded his capacity to participate in the life he cherished as father, spouse, brother, son, friend, law student, artist, athlete, and opera aficionado. Psychological pixilation (aka schizophrenia), in my father's case,[14] occurred over a five-year period in the late 1950s and early 1960s, decades comparatively in the dark ages in terms of effective approaches to mental health treatment and the social stigma associated with those afflicted.

In the beginning, Dad's leave-taking was subtle. I first felt a slight shift in relationship over the course of our vacation at the New Jersey shore during the summer of my seventh year. He was uncharacteristically moody, easily irritated, emotionally distant, and slept in a downstairs bedroom of the oceanfront beach house my grandparents rented. By fall of that year, he was hearing typewriters whisper disturbing messages as he walked the hallways of the law school he attended; later he began to act out idiosyncratic and unacceptable notions. Although he did not talk with me about his disturbing inner experiences (my mother told me years later), I remember feeling increasingly watchful around him, concerned for the safety of my younger brothers, my mother, and myself.

Over the course of the next several years, my father appeared to be riding a psychological roller coaster, in which he experienced precipitous declines, plateaus when we all enjoyed a respite, and even elevated periods when there was renewed hope for his complete recovery. He received the best psychiatric care of the day but eventually succumbed to the devastating symptoms and vanished into a parallel world of delusions, hallucinations, and inexplicable, unpredictable behavior. It was an increasingly uncertain, sometimes frightening time for all of us.

My rapport with my father was such that I was sometimes able to intervene during episodes when he was trapped in a reality all his own. I look back now and remember being acutely aware of our size and power differences and can imagine what David must have felt as he confronted Goliath. I was not encountering an adversary but my beloved dad, who was nevertheless potentially dangerous. My mission was to soothe his spirit, to draw him back from the "twilight zone" in which he seemed to vanish. In preparation, I prayed for strength, sensitivity to the subtleties of my dad's mood and thought processes, and the capacity to engage him through empathy. Awe was my companion.

Eventually, with strong professional advice to do so, my mother reluctantly obtained a divorce (uncommon in the early 1960s) in order to ensure a more secure and stable life for my brothers and me. Although necessary for our safety and well-being, the heartbreak experienced was similar in magnitude to a death in our family. Unlike a literal death, my dad's slipping away had no public or private ritual in which to say good-bye, acknowledge our mourning, or to receive sympathy. The stigma associated with a major mental health disorder around the midpoint of the twentieth century did not encourage disclosure or acknowledgment.

My father physically died three decades later from emphysema, probably related to his chronic smoking habit. When I was in my early twenties I met briefly with him twice, once while he was still residing in a state hospital (a looming, gothic institution in my eyes) and then after he was released and living in a halfway house. I had hoped to reestablish a relationship with him, optimistically thinking that he might wish to do so too. I quickly realized his persistent psychological suffering and experiences during years of treatment had rendered him incapable of such engagement. I am not certain that he knew me. He inhabited the physical shell of his former self, albeit older and thinner, but to my great sadness, all of the personal and relational qualities, and shared memories that made him "Dad" had evaporated.

The symptoms of schizophrenia are *awful* in their power to diminish the personhood of the individual afflicted and to fragment a family. My family members' sustaining and insulating love, and in very pragmatic ways, our socioeconomic resources significantly mitigated the awfulness of my father's particular manifestations of schizophrenia. Together, we valiantly succeeded in keeping our family vessel afloat, even though transiting uncharted, swirling, sea monster-infested waters. We were awesome in our heroic stances. Our combined coping strategies worked to fortify resilience in everyone but my father who increasingly seemed to bob just beyond our reach in the turbulence of his chaotic mind. Eventually, reserves depleted, we watched helplessly as currents too powerful and too deep for us to fathom or stem swept my father away.

As a child growing up in the midst of the maelstrom produced by my father's debilitating psychological decline, I drew inspiration and strength—resilience—from experiences in which I felt the buoyancy—the optimism—of awe. Even more profoundly, awe-enhanced moments offered an enlarged perspective on life, including its challenges and bombshells.

Through the portal of awe, I saw the world around me in Technicolor. I marveled at its grandeur and diversity, and felt simultaneously humbled and reassured. During this time, I not only had awe-inspiring experiences stimulated by the world around me but also vicariously through literature and the burgeoning medium of television. I traveled to fascinating places and met an array of fabulous animals with Marlin Perkins and Jim Fowler, hosts of *Wild Kingdom*. When I was a little older, David Attenborough of the British Broadcasting Corporation, Walt Disney Presents, and National Geographic contributed informative documentaries, and Jacques Yves Cousteau's exciting expeditions allowed me to dive beneath the sea. It was comforting to realize that my family and I were also members of the world's marvelous animal kingdom and like all creatures had both strengths and vulnerabilities, and were subject to the laws of nature. This realization lent perspective to my family crisis. I felt that we belonged, even though my father appeared, in the vernacular of the day, to "be going crazy," and we no longer fit the *Father Knows Best* (a popular television program) American family ideal. It is little wonder that as an adult, Beston's existential reflections about people and animals capture my imagination: We are all "caught . . . in the net of life and time" and are subject to "the splendor and travail of the earth."[15]

Implicit lessons about existential realities often emerged through my experiences of awe. For example, I remember feeling simultaneously thrilled and apprehensive by the sight and sounds of towering, foam-crested Atlantic breakers crashing upon the shore during summer northeasters at Mantoloking, New Jersey, and Nags Head, North Carolina. After the storms moved through, the tremendous forces at play were recorded in the wind-sculpted dunes, and the legion of shells and flotsam and jetsam tossed high up the beach (once, among the many treasures was a message in a bottle from the Woods Hole Oceanographic Institution). Although the forces of nature awed me in the old-fashioned sense of the word by their magnitude, unpredictability, and raw beauty, I learned that within them are also ancient rhythms, which served to reassure me. I realized that even the strongest weather systems blow through and eventually subside, and that I could count on the cyclical ebb and flow of daily tides, the phases of the moon, and changing seasons. Nature reminded me that I am sometimes powerless to change things, though I learned that I have the ability to choose my stance toward what life presents.[16] Such metaphors, dovetailed with the strengthening agents of faith, family, and friends, bolstered my courage, so that I could better face the profound loss occurring in my life.

When delusions and hallucinations overwhelmed Dad's capacity to cope and he acted out in alarming ways, I sometimes felt *awe-struck* by the extent of his metamorphosis. Reflecting back, I learned another important existential lesson: Receptivity to awe does not discriminate; it means being sensitive to a full range of awe-inducing human experiences—of being fully alive to what is so—even when it shakes the foundations of the world as I know it.

What else was awe-inspiring at seven or eight years of age? So many things prompted awe, as I think is common for children not yet taught to disregard the wonders around them or to dampen their enthusiasm. The miraculous stories of my faith background provided a wellspring of awe upon which to draw, as did the frequent, directly experienced extraordinary events of daily life. Springing to the fore in my fond memories, in addition to the examples given above, are the many nights of falling asleep to beautiful, impromptu classical and jazz piano concerts played by the teenage boy who lived across the street (our windows were open as air conditioning was not yet widespread). The music stimulated my imagination and deeply moved me to spiritual reflection and prayer. To my young ears, my neighbor's artistic skill was awesome, but it was the feelings of joy and comfort—that sense of "phoning home" (like the character E.T. of movie fame) and feeling connected to my Creator and to Life that sustained me in the face of my father's increasingly disturbing personality and behavioral changes. Again, I had glimpses of the bigger picture of existence and found it reassuring.

A significant occasion during this time in my life was the gift of my first dog, a charcoal black miniature poodle. Dogs had always been members of our family but she was extra special; she was the first dog entrusted to me. The mother of the talented pianist, an older friend with whom I often shared cinnamon toast on Saturday mornings, offered me the pick of the litter (although in actuality the puppy selected me) when her dog delivered eight healthy puppies. I thought the sight of the newborns nestled with their mother amazing and felt honored that my canine friend permitted me to be with her pups without expressing protective behavior. The meta-message conveyed by both friends was truly awesome: They loved and trusted me with this phenomenal new bundle of life; their accolade bolstered my psyche (heart, mind, and soul). The enormously affectionate, playful canine companion (a giant in a miniature dog's body) did too for the next fourteen years.

From my perspective, the quest for healing entails living a heroic life; it is an unfolding journey of mythic proportions. According to mythologist Joseph Campbell, "the goal of the hero trip down to the jewel point is to find those levels in the psyche that open, open, open."[17] Healing wounds acquired in relationship with a loved one troubled by a major psychological impairment is predicated on accessing the deeper levels in one's psyche and paradoxically, it serves as a key for gaining access. A complex, nonlinear process, healing also evolves in tandem with each developmental stage in life. For example, when I was a child, healing essentially meant soothing the raw edges of profound loss and grief, and restoring a sense of balance that let me know I was safe in the world. In adolescence, healing was focused on repairing self-esteem and "managing a spoiled identity" (a term coined by social psychologist Irving Goffman[18]), addressing the longing for Dad's return and the reconstitution of our family, and exploring the questions central to all teens, such as "Who am I?" and "Where am I going?" Simultaneously, I began to absorb and work through the effects of the earlier trauma. In adulthood, as my self-and-world boundaries have expanded, my concerns have evolved. Healing is multilayered and sometimes surprisingly nuanced. Intriguingly, I have discovered that as my psyche continues to open, healing reveals "gifts in the wound," reconciliation, and profound compassion. "There is always more," as James Bugental, echoing early-twentieth-century psychologist William James, frequently declared; I find that to be true from the vantage point of midlife and am awed.

KS: What specific role has awe played in your specialty?
FP: In many respects, awe is at the heart of my vocation—my "callings" as a psychotherapist and educator. I sometimes see my life under the auspices of awe in terms of shaping interests, cultivating sensitivities and abilities, and presenting opportunities. Certainly, I had preprofessional preparation toward becoming a therapist during my childhood. Were the ordeals associated with my father's confusion a "means for the soul's calling to come forth," as archetypal psychologist James Hillman might suggest?[19] I can only speculate but I find this idea, rooted in myth and mystery, to be intriguing. Hillman reminds us that the way we imagine our lives is vitally important, that it influences one's way of being in the world.

Intriguing too is the question of awe's role in cultivating my "specialty," not only as my vocation but also construed as my unique way of being in the world. Hillman suggests asking the following questions: "How am I useful to others? What do people want from me?"[20] The ongoing answers to these questions may yield insights as to special gifts drawn forth and tempered through life experiences, those full of awe and the awful. From this vantage point, it is possible to embrace it all.

Awe also plays a role in my choice of theoretical orientation as a licensed psychologist. I consider myself extremely fortunate to have come of age as the humanistic movement in American psychology was flowering. Liberating fresh ideas about human potential permeated the intellectual air I breathed throughout my education and training. The founding contributors to this perspective (e.g., Charlotte Buhler, James F. T. Bugental, Sidney Jourard, Abraham Maslow, Rollo May, Carl Rogers, Anthony Sutich) took issue with the dominant reductionist theories of the day, psychoanalysis and behaviorism, and broadened the interests of psychology as a science to include the full range of human nature, especially the "higher reaches," such as awe, peak experiences, self-actualization, love, truth, beauty, joy, the transpersonal, and the mystical. As Bugental wrote, these psychologists were willing to "truly encounter mystery" and shared the guiding principle of standing in awe of their subject matter, the human *being*.[21] The work of the pioneers inspired me, as does the work of contemporary contributors, who are responding to this generation's challenges and expanding the frontiers of knowledge and practice. The evolution of the humanistic perspective in psychotherapy continues under several rubrics, including existential-humanistic, person-centered, "emancipatory, experiential, existential-integrative, transpersonal, and contructivist."[22]

KS: What role do you see awe playing in the larger scope of society?
FP: Awe has the potential to be a unifying force. I recently saw evidence of such unity as I watched the spectacular athletic achievements and dedication to excellence exhibited by the participants of the 2008 Olympic Games in Beijing, China. Empathic resonance transcends cultural differences. Interestingly, the power of awe for promoting unity among nations or individuals does not capture the headlines or much media attention in general in our culture.

Kindred spirits seem to find one another through shared experiences of awe. Recently, I was standing with one of our dogs at the railing of the upper deck of a small ferry, keeping a close watch out for orcas, porpoises, seals, and other marine life that inhabit the waters I was transiting. A woman of about my age came to the railing beside me. Soon we were engaged in an animated conversation about our mutual fascination with orcas and other marine mammals. In the process, each of us disclosed the rather intimate feeling of receiving a gift—a blessing—whenever we see these stunning black-and-white animals in their natural environment. Although we did not see orcas during that brief ride, hearing highlights of her previous encounters with the resident pods[23] (family groups) was vicariously thrilling. The warmth of our empathic interaction, our shared awe, continued with me as we went our separate directions. Later that day I savored the spectacular sight of orcas, so "up close and personal" that the sound of their exhalations reverberated in my ears and off the rocks where I stood in the company of others equally captivated by these remarkable representatives of other realms. The joy and gratitude among the assembly of whale watchers was palpable. I believe such gracious feelings are contagious and yield dividends as they ripple throughout relationships.

A "natural high" is another positive by-product of experiencing events considered wondrous or awesome. Neuropsychologists tell us that these subjective feelings of well-being appear to be associated with the release of endorphins and other neurotransmitters in the brain. Our bodies seem designed to produce pleasure and ease pain. We wear the ruby slippers, but, just as it was for Dorothy in *The Wizard of Oz*, some of us do not recognize their inherent power and probably most of us would profit from learning how to maximize our endowment. Imagine the personal and societal benefits in terms of overall health, stress management, and expressions of goodwill if more people were under the influence of awe. Perhaps our contemporary culture would have less need of the artificial, sometimes harmfully addictive potions or troublesome compulsive behaviors that impede full-out living. Among people who model "kissing life fully on the lips"[24] (as world cruiser Fatty Goodlander puts it) is the poet Walt Whitman.

Whitman celebrated the natural euphoric feelings associated with seeing himself and the world through awe-colored lenses. An excerpt from "Song at Sunset"[25] included in the 1891–1892 edition of *Leaves of Grass*, communicates his zest; it is delightfully contagious.

Wonderful how I celebrate you and myself!
How my thoughts play subtly at the spectacles around!
How the clouds pass silently overhead!
How the earth darts on and on! And how the sun, moon, stars, dart on and on!
How the water sports and sings! (surely it is alive!)
How the trees rise and stand up, with strong trunks, with branches and leaves!
(Surely there is something more in each of the trees, some living soul.)
O amazement of things—even the least particle!

Emerson, whom Whitman admired, proclaimed, "The invariable mark of wisdom is to see the miraculous in the common."[26]

KS: How does awe contrast and compare with religion, psychotherapy, and other forms of recovery and healing in our society?
FP: The Hunter's Moon[27] (as it is known in some Native American traditions) is rising above the tapering tops of the luxuriant blue spruce trees in my backyard as I begin this section. The air is crisp and clear—fall is arriving. I feel such joy at being alive and partaking in the splendor of this spectacular October night. My senses are aflame and I am in awe of the natural beauty that encircles me. When the coyotes howl at midnight, I join them in celebration.

David Elkins, a humanistic psychologist, might call my moonlit revelry an example of "poignant moments," a common type of sacred experience along a continuum of intensity culminating in mystical encounters.[28]

Such poignant moments according to Abraham Maslow are "small mystical experiences," and are a form of "peak experience," which he defined as "transient moments of self-actualization" and "moments of ecstasy."[29] Maslow thought that almost everyone has these special experiences but that some people may not be cognizant of them or may discount them. He suggested that one of the responsibilities of psychotherapists is to "[help] people to recognize these little moments of ecstasy."[30] Doing so, Maslow hypothesized, facilitates the process of opening to one's full potential and full humanness.

Depth psychotherapists, physicians, clergy, mystics, shamans, sages, and others who honor personal experience draw upon the power of awe in their varied approaches to the promotion of recovery and healing, defined as, "to make sound or whole, to restore to health, or to cause an (undesirable condition) to be overcome."[31] Frank and Frank recognize *these* shared aims and methods among healers in their intriguing text, *Persuasion and Healing: A Comparative Study of Psychotherapy.*[32]

Awe appears to be a universal human phenomenon. Although many events commonly spark awe (e.g., an eclipse of the sun or moon, the birth of a child, the northern lights, exceptional courage), the actual experience of awe is distinctly personal. We each have unique inner responses to the same stimulus. Each of us attributes meaning to what we consider to be awesome based upon our current self- and world view. Degree of affiliation (or nonaffiliation) with a particular religious belief system contributes to the way awe is assimilated or even influences that which inspires awe.

Broadly defined, a religion is "a set of beliefs concerning the cause, nature, and purpose of the universe, especially when considered as the creation of a superhuman agency or agencies, usually involving devotional and ritual observances, and often containing a moral code governing the conduct of human affairs."[33] Spirituality, as Elkins[34] points out, is often distinguished from religion by being a more personal, private recognition of the sacred and expression of devotion. Both religions and individualistic spiritual paths provide lenses through which to perceive and interpret the world, including experiences of awe. For example, the spiritual philosophy of my Celtic ancestors is rooted in a joyful love of nature and a belief in the holiness of all Creation.[35] The world is ripe with awe from such a perspective.

Devotional acts and observances associated with religions often appear to have their roots in historical, shared experiences of awe. Their practice invites awe and harnesses its power to transform consciousness from the worldly to the spiritual. Examples of awe-based spiritual practices include, prayer, chanting, meditation, dancing and pilgrimages; ceremonies, such as dhikr (Sufi tradition), the lighting of the Hanukkah menorah (Jewish tradition), Holy Communion (Christian tradition), and the Buffalo Dance (Pueblo tradition);[36] and celebrations, such as Christmas, Eid ul-Fitr at the conclusion of Ramadan, Rosh Hashanah, and Diwali, the Hindu "Festival of Lights." Awe, inspired through participation in the sacred practices of one's religious or spiritual belief system, fans the flame of spirit, that vital, mysterious animating force within each of us that unites mind, body, and soul.[37]

Psychotherapy, like awe and our faith systems, has the potential to catalyze changes in our ways of being alive. All three may serve as agents of transformation, in that they each stimulate imagination, tap subjectivity, "our natural state and necessary place of refuge and renewal,"[38] and open perceptual boundaries. Bugental observes, "The agency of therapeutic change is the opening of perceptual boundaries—that is, seeing important aspects of our lives in fresh ways."[39] Imagination, the conceptual capacity to create enticing images of what is possible or desired, draws us forward toward actualizing our goals and allows us to more creatively meet the daily challenges and the emergencies of our lives.

One difference between awe and the process of psychotherapy is that the latter is a consciously undertaken enterprise between two people (or more in group therapy) and is typically initiated for the purpose of addressing the client's concerns. By comparison, awe is a spontaneous, surprising experience, although I am certain that for each of us there are places and situations more likely to invite the phenomenon. Engagement in "deep play," described by naturalist Diane Ackerman as an "ecstatic form of play" that involves "the sacred and the holy,"[40] provides such an invitation. Deep play takes many forms and its delights are enduring. A cherished deep play experience for me occurred while on a World Wildlife Fund[41] cruise several years ago, when the community aboard our small ship serendipitously shared a remote Alaskan cove with a pod of slumbering humpback whales. Much to the delight of all on board, the leviathans entered the cove as twilight turned to darkness and the heavens filled with stars; their sonorous, rhythmic breathing primarily revealed their presence. The whales' exhalations reverberated throughout the cove, through the hull of our vessel, and for me, forever within my being. Capping the splendor of the night was the ethereal light of the aurora borealis, its waves of luminous color transforming the northern sky into a watercolor canvas. As the need for sleep eventually overtook my excitement in the wee hours of the morning, I enjoyed the utter peace that comes from being in "harmony with the mysterious Spirit of the Universe."[42]

Psychotherapy is beautifully described by Ackerman as a form of deep play. It involves a sacred encounter and a sacred mission: the care, tending, and emancipation of the client's psyche "toward the farther reaches of human nature."[43] "Life changing psychotherapy," according to Bugental, "is the effort of patient and therapist to help the former examine the manner in which he [or she] has answered life's existential questions and to attempt to revise some of those answers in ways which will make the patient's life more authentic and thus more fulfilling."[44] The goals of healing and recovery are waypoints on the journey.

Maslow hypothesized that the potential to have peak experiences, "moments of ecstasy,"[45] is enhanced when we move beyond constant attention to meeting deficiency needs or enslavement to outdated defense mechanisms. In addition to enlarging one's life through greater authenticity, Maslow underscored the importance of cultivating "unitive perception" or "resacralization."[46] Rather than perceiving the world in a concrete linear fashion, resacralization involves "being able to see the sacred, the eternal, the symbolic."[47]

Resacralization colors one's entire psychic topography. This perspective supports the ability to "put your arms around what life presents, *all* that life offers."[48] I am reminded of Forrest Gump's famous line (in the 1994 movie) about life being like a box of chocolates, and not knowing quite what you'll get. As psychiatrist Irvin Yalom poignantly reminds us, "Everyone—and that includes therapists as well as patients—is destined to experience not only the exhilaration of life, but also its inevitable darkness: disillusionment, aging, illness, isolation, loss, meaninglessness, painful choices, and death."[49] Jon Kabat-Zinn, known for promoting the benefits of mindfulness meditation practice, encourages us to cultivate a "a way of being, a way of looking at problems, a way of coming to terms with the full catastrophe that can make life more joyful and rich than it otherwise might be."[50] Similarly, Viktor Frankl's Logotherapy, "an optimistic approach to life,"[51] encourages us to search for meaning in all of the circumstances with which we are confronted throughout our lives. "Logotherapy teaches that pain must be avoided as long as it is possible to avoid it. But as soon as a painful fate cannot be changed, it not only must be accepted but may be transmuted into something meaningful, into an achievement."[52] Psychotherapy, religious and spiritual belief systems, and other recovery and healing philosophies serve to guide and invigorate the transmutation process. Awe offers a font of meaning under the auspices of any of these guides. Alternatively, surprised by awe, one may be catapulted into a fresh, life-enlarging perspective, brimming with new meaning. I believe this is what Albert Schweitzer experienced as it became apparent to him that "reverence for life is a universal ethic."[53]

CANDICE HERSHMAN AND THE AWE OF UNKNOWING

Candice Hershman is a recent graduate of a master's program in psychology. She is also a colleague and former student. Although I have known Candice for several years, it is only recently that I realized the extent of her self-transformation. As with Fraser Pierson, awe has been a longtime "companion" for Candice. Her relentless curiosity and voracious spirit have persistently fueled her; and her acute sense of life's travails, with equal fervor, have consistently sobered her. Witness now the fruit of her discoveries, and the earthy, tangible lessons of her renewal.

KS: What does the notion of awe mean to you?
CH: For me, the experience of awe conjures up the feeling of being a small, separate entity, and yet significant somehow and

connected to the universe. I think there is a tendency for people to view significance as something large and obvious, rather than intricate and discrete. Still, it is the times when I am paying attention to the aspects of the world that typically go unnoticed that I feel awe.

Another aspect of awe that I feel is important involves an acceptance of not knowing, but appreciating in spite of this. I am not talking about ignorance, for that would be "ignoring," and awe requires paying attention. This experience involves a certain level of submission to the greatness of everything, yet ironically, amplifies the sense that when it comes to self-empowerment, life has been magnanimous in giving me free reign over my experiences. A good example of this is witnessing a severe thunderstorm. I have no control over which direction the clouds will move and when they will let down rain, lightning, or even a funnel cloud. Still, I can choose to ignore the rain and go about my business inside my home, turn on the weather channel, watch from the window, or take a risk and stand outside in the middle of the storm. Whatever choice I make in relation to the storm will alter my personal experience. Whatever attitude I have at the time will alter the choice I make. This explanation may seem complex, but in my experience, recognizing this sort of complexity is a distinct element of awe.

A final element of awe for me involves union of all parts of myself. When in awe, my body, mind, heart, and spirit all recognize and acknowledge each other. They may not all agree, but even dissonance qualifies as harmony. All parts of myself are stirring and acutely aware. I would take care to differentiate between awareness and knowledge here. When in awe, I am paying attention and am in relationship to my surroundings, but I don't necessarily know or understand. My experience may be ineffable, but I value the significance of the moment.

KS: What is the basis for your sense of awe?
CH: For me, the basis of awe lies in creativity (if asked how I worship, I would probably say with poetry and music). It seems that people who create are acutely aware that there is a mysterious

aspect of life slightly out of our grasp which only comes to light for us when we receive our muses. I believe that artists spend a considerable amount of time creating because it is one of the only ways in which we can bridge the gap between what we can't control or understand into a medium that will suffice. Medium brings up a few images for me. Some are a piano, a lump of clay, or the pen and paper. However, another image that comes to me is the swami with her crystal ball, evoking and channeling the spirits of our deceased loved ones, or exploring premonitions of what will happen in our futures. Whichever image we choose, the point is that the medium gives breath and a voice to the aspects of life that are just out of reach for us. In order for the artist to do this, she must engross herself in what it is that captures her attention and appreciate it in ways that we may not when just getting through the day. Some people may look at a still life and just see a bowl of fruit, dish towel, and an empty bottle, but an artist wonders about the light and shadows, the textures, the different shades, the relationship of the various objects with each other. The objects are not just there to toss out or devour, but have a life and meaning of their own that the artist is in awe of when painting them. They are still life.

Artists are not the only patron saints for creativity and awe. Raising children well is a creative act, as is coming to compromise on an issue that has no simple answer. Growing food and cooking a palatable meal involves creativity. These are just a few examples of acts that involve an appreciation for the complexity of a person, place, object, or idea.

I see relationships as another basis for awe. The first relationships I think of are the ones I have cultivated with my own children. I was surprised when I became a mother at everything I did not know or understand, as well as the many tender memories and pain that came up for me in navigating the road of parenting. Babies are not equipped with the language we adults are most fluent in, and we have to tune into them in a different manner. We have to become more intuitive and use more senses to relate to our children if we are to learn how to best care for them. My relationship with my children taught me how to be more in my body and increased my ability to be present to them in the moment. This new skill has translated into other areas of my life, including my work with children and clients. It involves a way of being more present in a full-bodied way which aligns the senses with thoughts and action. This is a gift I have received from my children.

Another relationship that I believe was a basis for awe is the relationship I have with my father. It is true that when I was young, he was not there for me in the way that he is today. My father avoided dealing with the abusive environment my mother and stepmother created by escaping through work. He was a kind man, but struggled with stepping up for me when I was young. My father and I have had to work hard at healing our relationship. However, as an adult I can look at the relationship I have now with my father and the positive experiences I did have with him as a child. My father has an enthusiasm for life and manner of looking at things and people through fresh eyes. I have noted over the years that a walk on the beach with my father is much akin to a return to childhood. He picks up the same type of seashell that I must have seen a hundred times in my life, and one would think that he just found the key to Davey Jones' locker. What comes to mind for me are the lines from the T. S. Eliot poem "Little Gidding" which speak of relentlessly exploring something—even for a lifetime perhaps—and at the end of all the searching getting to know that something as if it were the first time one laid eyes upon it.

This is the manner in which my father experiences the world, as if he is seeing something wonderful that he has never seen before, regardless of how many times we have been there. To me, this represents an aspect of awe that is crucial. It creates a feeling of timelessness.

The same is true in the way my father listens to a story that somebody is telling. He becomes completely engrossed and impressed with that person. My father has a way of making people feel special, and people love to be around him. I attribute that to his natural ability to perceive people as he does the world: in a state of awe.

When I was young, I wish my father could have been there for me in these ways more often than he was, but also see that the little time I did have with him made a large impact on my concept of awe. I think that this stands as a testament to the power that even brief encounters can have on a person.

KS: What role has awe played in recovery or healing in your life?
CH: Regarding healing, the role awe has played in my life evolves continuously.

I grew up in a chaotic, yet restrictive home environment with a great deal of drug and alcohol abuse, as well as physical, sexual, and emotional abuse. At that time, my frame for awe was Christianity. Although there was a dogmatic and punitive tone to religion when I was young, there was also a message of hope that I have not abandoned. That message entailed a master plan and a belief that if I was "good" and had faith, things would get better. However, my patience wore thin and in high school I sought comfort in drugs and people who did not genuinely care for me. I was pretty out of control, making some sketchy choices. I am certain that this is due to my lack of awareness of the darker elements of my being, a natural result of wanting so badly to be so "good."

I turned my back on religion, but eventually opened myself up to something I didn't understand. I paid attention to the signs that the world sent me (unfortunately it seems that these days people are at risk for being labeled psychotic if they place belief in these synchronistic experiences). Amazingly, the signs that I followed in the outer world were reflections of my inner world. They helped me appreciate and trust my intuition. That intuition has led me to believe in my own potential, which was contrary to the predominant messages I received about myself when growing up. I wouldn't have heard myself protest useless and damning messages if I wasn't tuning in and looking for the small wonders that helped me make sense of my own path.

I also sought out people who seemed to encompass the values that I unknowingly held in my gut. This involved risking rejection or disappointment. However, I have eventually learned to accept, tolerate, and even appreciate pain. Ironically, part of my healing involves knowing that I will never be complete or entirely whole, or in possession of this sudden great knowledge which will transform all of my relationships and safeguard me from adversity. I have come to realize that the day I am immune to pain and am completely "healed" is the day when I have become numb to life. Contrary to this, I believe that one cannot feel awe if one has not seen one's own wounds and accepted that scars are inevitable. For me, healing involves being in awe of my whole self, which requires great attention and appreciation of who I am, my shadow side not being an exception.

KS: What specific role has awe played in your specialty (e.g., as educator, therapist, etc.)?
CH: I formerly spent fourteen years working in early childhood education. This field is especially compatible with the concept of awe, particularly in terms of the improvement of the profession. Young children naturally live in a state of awe, because everything is so new to them. Just being born can be likened to visiting a different planet. Unfortunately, much of education is based on "knowing," which can negate this process of discovery. It seems as if adults are tragically deprived of awe-based experiences. The sacrifice of awe in favor of being "in the know" is occurring progressively at an earlier age. It seems that childhood (which to me, is all about awe) is becoming a brief phase in the history of human development.

As an educator, I have at various times felt tremendous pressure to compromise the well-being of my students by conforming to prefabricated standards that do not honor children as individuals, or the awe-based process that is essential to their learning in a well-rounded way. I fear that with the wave of universal preschool in the United States, early childhood education will be modeled after the primary school system (kindergarten through the sixth grade). Young children are being expected to be pre-reading in preschool, when in the past, that task was reserved for kindergarten. In my opinion, the foundation of a good education for young children involves developing relationships and providing an environment and interactions that are rich in opportunities to explore the self, the other, and the world at large. This helps feed curiosity, which is a major building block for teaching children that learning is an internally rewarding experience. Additionally, by developing a quality relationship with each child who enters my classroom, I am modeling curiosity and wonder. How? Because a true relationship with each child involves an encounter that is unjaded by my preconceived notions about their world and what I am capable of doing (or not doing) in the classroom. I need to be inquisitive about who the child is. When I approach my job in this manner, I restore awe for the child and myself simultaneously. To me, it seems that this is the most effective way to heal the field of early childhood education, or preserve its obvious value.

KS: How does awe contrast and compare with religion, psychotherapy, and other forms of recovery and healing in our society?
CH: As a therapist in training, I believe that the concept of relationship is vital. Therapy is becoming more about pharmaceuticals and efficient techniques that only promote a "pseudo" version of health, and less about healing through a patient process of other/self-discovery. The relationship seems to be the best way to preserve the benevolence of the therapeutic profession. If each person who serves our community in a healing capacity could remember to treat each client with whom they come in contact as an individual, and infuse genuine curiosity about their clients into their work, they will be more capable of accessing the benefits of awe. Once again, the benefits of awe are caring and humble encounters which can transcend the weight of paper pushing and time lines. I believe that even brief encounter, when awe based, can have a restorative effect on the therapeutic profession. As a therapeutic preschool teacher who worked with children experiencing homelessness, I witnessed remarkable growth, healing, and change in just a few months with many children. I have no doubt in my mind that the healing was due to holding each child I was privileged to meet in a state of awe.

Regarding religion, I somehow feel that due to fixed attitudes about prophecy and righteousness, as well as a hierarchical organization in many places of worship, the most fundamental aspects of awe and wonder have been marginalized severely. Any time our attitudes about something are fixed, we are operating from a place that reveres static answers to mutable questions. We do not open ourselves to more information and relating to others. How can we attain wisdom with this stance?

Additionally, the notion that anybody has a greater capacity than another to relate to God or the cosmos seems presumptuously precocious. When we do this, we are losing sight of one of the most important aspects of awe, which is our smallness in the much larger scheme of being alive. Many leaders have lost sight of humility, and obtusely exploited their leadership roles in faith. I somehow suspect that these people were not called to the clergy, but rather were drawn to it by the lures of power.

KS: What role do you see awe playing in the larger scope of society?
CH: Just recently, Hurricane Katrina hit Louisiana and devastated the South. This is not the first natural disaster that has hit the United States or the entire world this year. We have had many massive hurricanes, a tidal wave, etc. . . . Every time something like this happens in the world, people seem shocked, yet it happens every year somewhere (more this year than for a while, still).

From what I understand, much of the tax money that could have been spent to build levees and safeguard the South was spent rather on instigating disaster in Iraq. Although I somehow believe that the war on Iraq is about revenue for corporate interests, I am going to play devil's advocate and speak in the context of terrorism and nuclear threats being the central reason behind war. Our U.S. leaders have spent billions of our tax dollars on an endeavor to create safety for our country, and yet nature has swept in and left us in devastation and a state of great loss. There is suffering right here before our eyes, and yet somehow our leaders have chosen to patronize anybody who cares as a proverbial bleeding heart who needs to get back into their head. Why do our leaders ignore real suffering? Why do they make war?

Paul Tillich suggested that neurosis is a response or attitude to a situation that works to the disadvantage of the one concerned—doing the opposite of what needs to be done. If I were to use this definition, I would say that our leaders are deeply neurotic, because the way to avoid terrorism is not to destroy a country and create more hatred toward our country. Where does this neurotic response come from? I believe from fear of our own mortality and ignorance of our humble position in relation to nature and the cosmos. It seems it would be even more challenging for a person in a powerful position to admit their ultimate lack of power. Our leaders have forgotten their smallness, and the atmosphere, bedrock, and ocean seem to feel the need to keep them in check.

So, how is this anecdote relevant to awe and society at large? It puts the need for awe into a context that cannot be altered (although I am sure that there are people out there trying—or not trying—to alter the atmosphere). We cannot do away with natural disasters. There is a place for powerlessness in life. I wonder if people who have the power to make a difference would be more capable of choosing the battles worth our while if they were more in touch with their vulnerabilities as beings that live on this planet, versus being men or women in suits with fancy titles and a knowledge of how the legal system and bureaucracy work. What is happening in the world today is almost mythical. If there were a book of wisdom to be handed down through the ages, this would be one of the most significant stories.

I was speaking the same day of Hurricane Katrina to an elderly woman who was labeled schizophrenic, and she continually spoke of the ark of Noah and the flood. I felt so much awe in listening to her—it was almost prophetic, and made me wonder just how "crazy" she really was. People thought that Noah was a fool for paying attention to the voice of God, but he built an ark. Noah must have been a man who knew about awe. He paid attention to the signs, the rainbow, and the dove with the olive branch. Today we have signs—scientists telling us that global warming may be responsible for many of the disasters we are facing, and many ordinary people who are concerned as well. It seems foolish to me that most politicians don't care about this. They are numb to the real suffering, and therefore don't know how to prevent it. They are not in awe. Too bad for the rest of us.

KS: Is there anything else you would like to add about awe-based recovery or healing?
CH: I am not sure that awe is an experience, but rather a quality of an experience, or a way of being. I would say that awe is essential to wonder, and vice versa.

Regarding recovery or healing—I am not sure there is such a thing. I think that quality of life may be a more useful term here. Although pain and defenses may keep us from noticing certain elements of both our internal and external worlds, eradication of pain and defenses could blunt our capacity to appreciate their inherent value, thus numbing us to joy and awe. It is hard to experience awe when we are so focused on one aspect of our lives. I think perhaps being able to integrate new experiences and perceptions into our worlds can help us assimilate our memories of suffering and transform them. This requires awe in the sense that we must be willing to take a look around and be absorbent. I also believe that if we can somehow marry subjectivity and objectivity in a phenomenological sense when observing ourselves and the world (I guess this would be the observing ego), we may have a greater capacity to tap awe, and subsequently honor our pain and its alchemical qualities.

6

AWAKENING FROM DRUG ADDICTION

I've known Michael Cooper for close to twenty years. He's been a great friend and confidant. He's also been the quintessential spokesman for dark nights of the soul. Michael is a summa cum laude graduate of the Graduate Theological Union of Berkeley, California (1994). He is also a yoga instructor, a case worker, and a loving, "equal opportunity" minister to friend and stranger alike.

As of this writing, Michael is fifty-seven years old. When he was thirteen, his mother committed suicide. At twenty, following his breathtaking Olympic-bound stint as a gymnast, Michael abruptly discovered the death and possible suicide of his brother; and by twenty-five, Michael too had virtually succumbed—not to physical death, but the spiritual bankruptcy of drugs.

And then Michael rediscovered awe . . .

MICHAEL COOPER AND AWE-BASED REHAB

KS: What is your notion of awe?
MC: When we begin to break down the cultural stories about what should be and what is truly spiritual or clever or sophisticated, then I like to just [get] down and get real. . . . I'm reasonably intelligent but I'm not Mensa quality, so I try to make my strong suit just telling it like I see it.

So in terms of what you had described [in an earlier conversation] as the "atrophy of awe," . . . my experience is that we are so starved for the sense of awe that we look outside of us for something we can buy or rent to experience [it], instead of seeing [it] in a sense of astonishment, in our awareness of being itself, in the fact that what is, is. Byron Katie talks about this in terms of "loving what is"—and I think about it as being blown away by what is.[1]

One of my earliest memories, probably [at] about four or five, as I was standing outside our family home in Menlo Park, was looking at this trellis of roses and seeing and feeling the wind blow through my hair and through the foliage of the roses, and looking up at the sun, and having that raw sense of awe.

We're malnourished. We're starved and thirsty for that basic raw material of awe. And how do we increase that . . . except, as Jesus said, by becoming like little children again. And that doesn't mean . . . regressing in our intelligence. But it does mean we're all beginners here. It's Zen mind, beginner's mind; and when we get to that place how can we have anything but astonishment?

One of the things, again, that I remember as I got older is that social expectation of how I was supposed to be—smart or clever or well accomplished. And that kind of thing began to erode that sense of awe. For instance, instead of just being amazed at how a machine works or in awe of the sunset or sunrise, we're supposed to figure it out. We're supposed to be masters of the technology instead of per-ceivers first. And to me, awe is the antidote to the . . . feeling [of] "oh, been there, done that." Because see, in our society, it is important to make that clear: "oh, I've been there and done that!" Whereas [in a culture of] being a natural mystic—like St. Francis—cultivating that sense of being blown away is the goal of life. It's not to cover it over and paste it over with expertise. It's almost as if we're technocrats of the imagination. We've subverted and co-opted the imagination so that we can predict it.

And what I'm all about in my checkered career and unpredict-ability is cultivating that sense of . . . well, in a sense: of being *out* of control. In my history, it's been both: in a negative way and a positive way. I'm just ranging here, but from *The Lord of the Rings*,

I think a lot of people can relate to that story, but there are several times when Gandalf the wizard sits down the little hobbit and says, "I know this is going to sound discouraging, but I don't have any idea how this [conflict with the ring] is going to turn out, and you don't have any idea of how things will turn out either." And I think that really speaks to American expertise . . . that reductionist certainty is such an addiction that we'd rather be certain that things are fucked up than to contemplate the possibility that we don't know, and that the end of the story has not even been written yet.

KS: Like we're certain about terrorists . . .
MC: Exactly. Well, you know, one of the first things after 9/11 our politicians were saying, "Those dirty bastards!" And one of the things I remember was that one of the really clever put-downs to anybody who spoke about justice rather than revenge was "so, what are you going to do, sit down with these terrorists and have an encounter group?" Well, why the fuck not, you know? I mean . . . the people on those planes, both the terrorists and the terrorized, had encounters of different levels of intensity and awe. I really love the story about the people who just got up and said, "screw you" [to the terrorists], "you're not going to crash this [plane] into the White House . . . we're going to stop you, and if we need to go down with you, that's fine." But . . . that's just where the adventure begins. . . . This kind of believing that "the terrorists will just sit still and everything will be fine" attitude won't work—it's not going to be fine. We have to test the waters more. We can't assume we're going to die, but we can't assume we're not going to die. We need to explore further. Hence, Zen mind, beginner's mind.

KS: Step out of the box?
MC: Exactly. And that's what those people did, the ones that crashed in Pennsylvania. We'll never know exactly what the dialogues were or what they were thinking, but absolutely they weren't listening to the terrorists like you're supposed to be listening to pilots, like "just strap in and you'll be fine, we'll take care of you." See, that's the part that I think [makes] us so fearful of terrorists: [the idea] that in a

way we can be terrorized by anybody or anything that challenges our beliefs, challenges our sense of safety. And the terror is at least as much contained in our response as it is in whatever violations and trespasses the "terrorists" present us with.

And the other thing is that we're terrified by having this mirror put up to us by certain peaceniks, and that's not at all to let the people who perpetrated 9/11 off the hook—it's not about that. It's about taking responsibility and seeing that part of why we're so scared of terrorists—I think—is because we see ourselves in there; that we see our own sense of mortality and danger . . . and violence [in them].

The issue of projection [regarding the above] is huge. And the sense of awe is being filled by what is rather than taking what is and then projecting it "out there."

In some ways [we're] afraid of being filled. [But what's] "awe-full," or "awesome," [is] being swept away by the magnitude of what's going on, whether it's a sunset, a terrorist act, a Jesus-walking-the-earth-again, a little child taking the time to help another child who stumbles in a race—there's so many awe-inducing experiences.

KS: That's a beautiful way to put it; can you expand on how . . . being blown away by the magnitude of an experience affects a person or affects you?
MC: In the language of my growing up in the '60s, as in "blowing the mind," and [your reference] in "Horror and the Holy" about hyper-constriction and hyper-expansion—see, that's . . . a big part of the whole thing. The world is hyper-constrictive and hyper-expansive, and there's something in our hardwiring that's really terrified of that. Of course you and I would say, "That's great!" [laughs]. We love horror movies! Because that's the type of thing that brings the intensity [to living]!

So to me, this is really huge stuff. We talk about God-fearing people . . . it's not just that God is going to put you through hellfire and brimstone . . . it's that God is awesome, and there's a part of us called the ego that doesn't like the concept that there's awesome realities out there, that are mysteries: unexplainable and paradoxical. So we end up, I believe, terrorizing ourselves with the need to make up stories to cover up the uncertainty and awe of this universe. So that when something like 9/11 comes along that's so disorienting, the first thing we have to [declare] is "those bastards!"

And the only thing you can do to cover it up is to project it out there [at the terrorists]. Because what makes it so horrific is that this is a mirror, a window on the state of our human being. It's not about Arabs and Americans, or Whites and Blacks, it's about . . . "oh my God, this is horrific." And something I really feel strongly . . . is that we're hyper-constricted in our foreign policy, in our theologies, in our political economy—it's like it's either us or them. It's not a sense that "this is [messed up], what are we going to do about this together?"

And I think that's one of the things that can be helpful to me and our friends out there, is to not cave in to the fear of terrorism, but also not to be a victim [and particularly not to] be a psychic victim to terrorism, where you become that which you hate.

KS: So you're saying that awe helps us to come together?
MC: Yes, awe can create an opening. And sometimes, certainly for me, awe creates this gaping wound of openness, so I have to check myself before I start filling it in with certainty. So what it brings to mind is that in the earthquake of '89, and then again in 9/11, there were times where the cataclysms opened a sense of community. 'Cause we're all [in this boat together]. We're all mortal. And I saw some of that in nascence, both times, but I think it got buried much more quickly following 9/11 because it was to the federal government's benefit to keep everybody afraid, than to open lines of communication. Whereas with the earthquake, it was San Francisco, and who cares about California, anyway? So that's one of my conspiracy theories, is that the government filled in with that counterterrorism [notion]. And when you're doing counterterrorism, how can you not say that you're also a terrorist; as opposed to Jesus being a counterterrorist or Gandhi being a counterterrorist, or Martin Luther King being a counterterrorist? That's a counterterrorist of a different sort.

So again that's where the projection comes in. If we respond to situations that are beyond comprehension, like 9/11, if there's that sense this is unexplainable, it's not logical, that can either be an opening for a sense of awe, and maybe a regrouping as a whole tribe of human beings rather than people who project things onto each other and look for scapegoats. It could be a real opportunity. But we're not trained that way. We're trained to be certain . . . to [adopt] empirical science, and to be sure of this and that, and if you take away that surety, then we're really terrorized. . . . [Yet] we're left in this awesome chasm and we're left with, "OK, what's next?" rather than, "OK, what's next is that we bomb the entire world until we're not afraid anymore."

And I do think that that's why Americans are so technique-oriented, and there's nothing wrong with that, but . . . technocracy assumes an idolatrous place where salvation comes from certainty, rather than a higher power that is larger than life. . . . It's . . . the sacred, it's spiritual, it's awesome, we're awestruck [before it]. And the difference is that when you're open to being awestruck, or as C. S. Lewis says, "surprised by joy," then you open yourself to an incredible power, a higher power, but you also open yourself to this awesome chasm of uncertainty, of mystery, of lack of control, and for those of us who have morbid control issues, it's really hard. It's like putting down an addiction, an addiction to control uncertainty.

KS: How is that important to you, to develop that lack of control [MC laughs here], that openness, and that surprise?
MC: It's the question of my life because . . . well, let's make it very specific to me. One of the particularly awe-filled moments was when I was thirteen and my dad came into my bedroom and said, "Your mother's dead." She committed suicide. And we didn't really have the skills in the early '60s . . . nobody really heard about the grieving process and having to go through shock and denial and anger and acceptance, that kind of thing. So I felt like I was stunted for many, many years. . . . Kind of like a dwarf tree, you know? And it has provided me "grist for the mill," the "creative irritant" (according to Jung) that prompted my system to develop more of the pearl of my soul.

But if I were to go back there and revisit that, I'm not all that certain I would do anything different. Instead of running away from the *vastness*, the *awesomeness*, I no longer had a mother anymore. This person whom I was so dependent on was no longer there. It was around the time of the "God is dead" theology, and there was this emptiness.

KS: What was your religious background at the time?
MC: We were brought up in the Methodist church. And my mother always predicted I was going to be a minister, because I had told her about my perception of awe in the wind and the sun and the rose-bushes. So I had a spiritual takeoff platform, but there's no cultural support, no crowd at the launching of this spiritual being, so it was like an aborted mission for a long time, and a couple of the things that I used to fill the hole of my soul were drugs—and before drugs, hyper-accomplishment at school.

KS: You were an overachiever?
MC: Yes, an overachiever in the sense . . . of [being an] overevaluator of the soothing balm that accomplishment gave me. It gave me relief from the awful feeling of being abandoned.

[It manifested] as trying to be smarter, more popular, or skill-ful—especially the Olympic striving [in gymnastics]. And that's why I fight this stuff so much in myself and other people, because if it worked I'd be selling it. But I've tried it for so long, and it's fool's gold. And it's very much like drugs.

After I had all this superachievement and had a full scholarship at the University of Oklahoma, and [was] on the Olympic track, then my brother was taken away from me . . . and [it was a] mysterious accident. They didn't know whether it was suicide or homicide, and they didn't have any answers for us.

So at that point I dipped into my first full-fledged depressive epi-sode. It was like I had gotten over the sense of . . . my mom [being] gone. . . . And I had felt cheated, and like in that song in that era, "Is that all there is?" I felt, "if that's all there is, my friend, let's keep on dancing. Let's break out the booze." And so I tried [following my mother's death] to reestablish my golden cord with existence and to fashion a compromise with God through this new being of a man of accomplishment. And then it was the double whammy. I had worked for four years to build this new structure and then I received the news about my brother, and then I went into a tailspin.

Probably one of the most important things for me was to finally allow myself to be falling. It's almost vertigo in the sense of like, "Where do I belong?" "Where's my God?" "Where's my family?" Because my family disintegrated around me.

KS: So this is the beginning of your sense of awe, the horrifying part?
MC: Yes, this is the horrifying part. This is the "out-of-control" [part] . . . the "dark night of the soul." It's so painful that it's always really hard to be authentic and to really understand how helpless and hopeless, and how depressed we can be, and yet still take another breath. See, that's it, that's the beginning. It's not, "OK, we have a fix here." We don't have a fix! There was this phrase in seminary, kind of a spoof on "I'm OK, you're OK," kind of a spoof on transactional analysis. . . . In one way the theological approach is "you know what, I'm *not* OK, and you're probably not OK, either. . . . And that's OK."

KS: Sounds like . . . you had a double vision there; that there was a piece of you that still had a sense of something more [than the quick fix].
MC: Yes, and it was that transition period. I said that the depression was very important to go through. I'm not a big advocate of "no pain, no gain," but there's no question in my mind that some of our most painful moments are some of our most growthful moments. And so I was in free-fall for a year. I gained a bunch of weight. I transferred from the prestigious university and came back home to the good old San Jose State University. Got involved in politics of protest, civil rights, and anti-Vietnam war kind of thing. So it was very rich, but I was just in free-fall. And I remember there were times when I'd listen to Simon and Garfunkel's "Search for America." [MC sings:] "We're all off to search for America." And I really became a deeper person because of [all] that. It was like I had my books and my poetry to protect me . . . that fortress of solitude inside. And that needed to be part of my seasoning process. I'm realizing . . . that we

wouldn't know who we *are* if we didn't know who we *were*. And it's so concise and so simple; it's so obvious [that] I was struck with a sense of awe [over that]. That sense of acceptance, and not—"OK, well now we understand!" [To the contrary,] I felt fucked and I still feel fucked and I'm OK with that, for the moment.

KS: It allows you to be what you are.
MC: Exactly . . . that is my sense. So . . . I had that quick fix of accomplishment and then that crashed and burned and then I floated for a year, with no fix. I didn't do drugs, and I didn't "do accomplishment." I had opened myself up to these new realms of radical politics, and humanistic psychology, and poetry, and lyrics and music and that kind of thing.

Then after that, it's not so clear. What began to arise was that I still wanted to do gymnastics but I didn't have to be the best. I didn't have to go to the Olympics. . . . And at points in order to get my weight down, so that I could enjoy gymnastics again, my girlfriend's uncle was a pharmacist and I had an unlimited supply of Dexamil, which was a very strong diet pill.

And that [weight gain] was another way to fill the hole in my soul. . . . So this diet drug, it's medical, you know, it has all the trappings of American technique, technocracy [he laughs]. It's like "Oh, you're not feeling up to par, forget about looking at the depths of terror that I felt . . . to really, really integrate that mom was not around," [but take the pill]. And it's like this wonderful pill allowed me to do better in my studies, took away my appetite, and . . . I could never have predicted this, [but] it took away my depression.

That [process] may be more obvious in these times, because people talk about depression more, but back then that [depression] was my secret, and all of a sudden it was like redemption. Somebody had come down and touched me and said, "You're healed, my son."

KS: A very powerful seduction.
MC: Yes, exactly. And that's why I'm very much opposed to the seduction of our youth, that seduction of our adults, in these easy fixes.

KS: Could you say a little more about how the fuller sense of awe opened up for you?

MC: Part of it was that I began to have these senses. There was this drug called MDA—kind of like Ecstasy [but] more powerful, more psychedelic—so it: was like a body psychedelic. And I was having these realizations of the larger [sense of awe]. I'm not going to make any bones about it; LSD, MDA, and mescaline definitely were one of the shapers back then [inspired by] Aldous Huxley's "Doors of Perception," and all of Alan Watts, and that kind of thing.

But when I look back on it, Kirk, talk about terrorism, talk about living on the edge of danger all the time [these experiences invoked that]. So paradoxically, my struggle with my depression over my mother's death, and my struggle with substance abuse forced me to break open into a whole new vault, completely different from anything I had tried to mine before. And one of the keynote distinctions [with many societal antidotes], was that yes, it touched and comforted these awful feelings but it was not a quick fix. And [also] it [didn't imply] that [things] get fixed and they stay fixed. Because I went through this place over and over again where I think I had a pretty good spiritual relationship to myself and the greater mystery of awe, and then that rascal depression would come in again—I'd gain weight and so on.

KS: So these solutions worked temporarily . . . and yet they opened you to other dimensions that kind of formed templates for later experience or possibility?

MC: Yes, well, one of the templates was, is, that it's a process, not a product. That's the good news and that's the bad news. And that's really a part of my theology, that Jesus and God are not going to come sweeping down here and fix me, but they will be *with* me. Their presence is very much felt both in my conscious times and unconscious times. There's this story called "Footprints," where this person looks back at his life and sees that Jesus and he had been walking along the sand together, and there's this point where there's only one set of footprints instead of two sets of footprints. And he says, "Why after all the faith I had in you, did you leave me?" And

Jesus said, "You misunderstand, my son: that was when I *carried* you!"

Again it's that poignancy. In a way, Siddhartha (later to become the Buddha) also has to deal with that "empty-nest" syndrome where he has to abandon his father and wife and family and his whole way of life and strike out on his own. And I do believe that we *all* need to do that. And again, it's not all that clear-cut—like "self-reliance" and the "American way" and all that. No, it's a very mysterious combination. It's a recipe that works for each of us in different ways at different times of our lives.

KS: *It's not linear.*

MC: Exactly, it's cosmic and it's ever-present, but you totally can't predict it. You can count on grace, but you can't predict it. You can't control it, you can't quantify it. You can't reproduce it on demand.

It's the balm of mystery. A part of us, our "monkey mind," looks at that mystical, cosmic, mysterious, awesome power as the enemy. Again the parallel between drugs and the quick-healing fixes that America and this culture offer because they don't understand the problem. They can't give the real fix—which is soul, which is paradox, which is bemusement, puzzlement, and awe and wonder and fascination, and horror, . . . and those intensities. It's like Valium is the solution rather than diving and doing a survey of the literature of horror and the holy.

KS: *Can you say more about what helped you to be able to open up to that paradoxical experience in a new way?*

MC: Yes, slogans are very valuable to me. Clichés become clichés because usually they make sense [laughs]. So one of the crises of faith that I've had . . . and it wasn't until many years later that I saw this as my salvation . . . is that sometimes "my ego is not my amigo." And to me, that's the breakdown right there.

My true conversion experience was finally saying out loud that I cannot rely on my ego to pull me out of things. That problem-solver, that fixer, that technique, that [idea] that all I have to do is find a particular lifestyle and then I don't have to deal with the awe and the horror of existence [—all that shifted].

KS: *The idea that all you have to do is "figure it all out."*
MC: Yes, and that's the ego's job, in my mind. And at that point, higher power, God, spirit, the divine take on less of a fearful quality versus, "All right! Bring it on!" Because my own experience is that I had an ingrained resistance to grace, to awe. . . . Again . . . often what we do when we're in trouble is to do the same thing over and over and harder and harder, instead of . . . breaking open to surrender or acceptance as Paul Tillich says, of the mystery or incredible awe of life.

To be very specific, it's not [complete] letting go of the ego, but letting go of my *reliance* on the ego, my *dependence* (like a drug) on the ego, and that's it. . . . To me . . . the ultimate idolatry is worshipping the ego, this monkey mind, rather than accepting that we have this ego, we have this busy monkey mind that's so sure it's right, that we . . . just assume that this is us, and that true salvation—"the only way we're going get through this"—is by ourselves, and that's our American way. . . . It's [about] tactics; we just have to figure out the right strategy.

But what I have come to believe is that the ego, the monkey mind, is a useful servant, but it's an awful boss because . . . our small self [ego] has no business running the show. However, we also don't have any business trying to exterminate it [or] exterminate the ego, or our materialistic feelings. [M then holds up a monkey doll and says:] This is my alter ego, he's my monkey mind, and I've learned to become very fond of him in his endearing qualities, but I'm not going to take any shit from him either when he starts trying to run my life!

KS: *In a sense [the monkey] is a part of the awe, but he's not the whole thing itself.*
MC: Exactly. And if I could break it down to its simplest, once I can get over myself as God, as the fixer, I can see that dynamic more clearly in other people and begin to accept that that's . . . an

ongoing project with each one of us, any relationship is; it's like a marriage.

KS: Can you say more about what you let go to, what you mean by God, and how that compares/contrasts with the more traditional view of God and . . . the view you experience in your AA (Alcoholics Anonymous) meetings?

MS: I'll try my level best [laughs]! Twelve-step philosophy and theology have been very instructive for me, although I have to say that I'm not a twelve-step fundamentalist, just like I'm not a Christian fundamentalist or a Yoga fundamentalist, or an intellectual fundamentalist. But one of the things they [AA] taught me, was that phrase. "My ego is not my amigo." I mean they say "my ego is not my amigo" like it's my enemy. I don't go along with that [extreme]. Sometimes, I assume my ego is my amigo and sometimes it's not . . . not that it's evil, but that it sometimes keeps me blind to other resources besides my own cleverness.

So Edward Kurtz wrote two books, one you're familiar with, *The Spirituality of Imperfection*, but he wrote an earlier book—actually a Ph.D. treatise—called "Not God." And that's a big AA concept. One of the things you first got to start with [in AA] is that there is a God, there is a higher power, and you're not it! [Laughs heartily.] [Yet], one of the wonderful things about [a] twelve-step [program] is that it peels you down at times that you can't really look at yourself—not because you're a hero, not because you're a drug addict or an alcoholic—it's just that there are times when the truth is sitting there staring you in the face and you have to say, "Oh, yeah, that's the elephant in the living room."

So the "not God," plus "my ego is not my amigo," leads me to the theology that God is not ego. That we're not God, and God is not ego. And it's kind of a reverse conversion experience, of finally letting go of that last tenacious grip of somehow "I'm going to fix it, and it couldn't possibly be something beyond my fathoming, beyond my power." So that's what really broke me open to higher power, [which] is just another name for something we don't understand, mystery, and awe—and again being surprised by joy, by grace, not through works, but just because we're blind lucky.

So a lot of my spiritual questing in my growing maturity is really calling myself on my tendencies to try to be God, and to [avoid] challenge. . . . God is not a super-talented ego, but is a letting go of concrete certainties we hang onto.

KS: So these are some of the negative qualities of God, but can you say more about what God is and how it differs from the traditional view?
MC: My experience of some forms of fundamentalism is that they want to get to that place of comfort and joy, without going through the awful, the horrific realization that we're not God. And we don't speak about that because that's the most sacrilegious, idolatrous thing we could do is have our ego, our monkey mind trying to run rampant. But in my humble opinion that's exactly what all of us are dealing with. Most of us, most of the time are afraid to acknowledge the following paradox: We know in our hearts that God is real and ego is illusion, but we live our internal lives thinking God is fiction and ego is fact!

The belief part of faith in the head trumps the mysterious faith of the heart and the belly and the groin, and the big toe. And then coming back up, all of those mysterious, unpredictable powers, and how they intersect and synergize with mind. And so all of a sudden instead of having exterminated the monkey mind, you've brought the monkey mind on board, and then from there there's tremendous power.

What I see in fundamentalist politics and fundamentalist religion is finding something that will fill the hole in the soul and saying, "That's it." Like, "Believe in me, and you shall have everlasting life;" or on a different level, instead of attacking the fundamentalists all the time, [I think of] drug addiction where I was sure that I needed more speed or cocaine, and that that was the answer. . . . Or in American democracy, "we just need a regime change and everyone will be like us." Well, talk about idolatry! Talk about arrogance!

So at that place where we have this sickening, this "sickness unto death," as Kierkegaard might say, [the sense of] despair and just being blown away by . . . that crushing realization that I first had when my mother took her life [is all somehow necessary]. It's all in the literature, we pay lip service to it all the time . . . we have to go through this crisis of faith, this dark night of the soul, this emptiness, in order to get to the fullness. We can't fill it up and make it OK. . . .

In Christianity there is "kenosis," which is the concept of self-emptying, creating a vacuum in our soul, which was previously clogged with certainty . . . so that we may at last be totally filled by the spirit of God. But you can't take a small mind, like we all have, and just blow it up like a balloon with certainty, and thus obviate the need to go through the "dark night of the soul." The theme of realizing that my mother's not God; Bush is not God; money is not God. We have to go through that negative to get to the positive.

AA is so simple that there's nobody too stupid to get it, but there's a lot of people too smart to get it. And it's seductive because you go, "Oh yeah, that [message about giving oneself over] is so right." Because my monkey mind has ruled me so much, but [that egotism] is not our solution, it's Bill's [the founder of AA] solution. And it becomes another absolute: "Just don't drink, and you'll be OK." Well, that's trash. Once I began to not handicap myself totally with drugs, then there's the . . . opening where real spiritual growth can happen. But there is this institutional momentum, inertia, that I see everywhere—in AA, in religion, in politics—"Just believe and everything will be OK," you know?

And that doesn't mean to me, "Don't believe." But I don't believe that that's the whole answer! And that's the part that letting go [becomes a problem]. Because I don't think my ego has the capacity to let go of that need for certainty, so I have to just deal with it . . . I need to figure out a way. . . .

KS: To live with the need, rather than punishing yourself for it . . .
MC: Exactly, and to me that's the stepping off the cliff . . . there's absolutely fear involved. To me anybody that says they have no fear . . . that's bullshit. If I said that to myself [bellowing], "I'm not afraid anymore!" that would be bullshit, and my small mind is so opinionated that if you told me that I'd tell you you're full of shit

[laughs]. But the only thing I can really know for sure is that the fear and sense of emptiness . . . those are very real. Those are just as real pitfalls and dangers and snares as pit bulls [who have been mortally wounding people in the Bay area of late]. So just like the pit bull—we don't exterminate [it], but maybe they're not the best household pet. And you don't have to be anti-dog to see that. It's like, people have had lions and leopards for pets—I don't think they should be killed, but I still don't think it's a very good idea [to keep them as pets].

So again, [it is important] not to demonize the ego, but also not to worship it. Those are two sides of the same coin. Like worshipping and just assuming that all people want to be like Americans and be consumers and be driven by ego fear, and blah, blah, blah, that's idolatry. But if you go to the other side and say, "Oh, there's only one way to deal with this, and just throw [that chauvinism] out!" that's not the way God has made this universe either.

KS: Yeah, that would be like throwing the monkey out with the bath-water.
MC: Exactly. . . . In Yoga lore, one of the tricksters we have to deal with is our monkey mind. Just like if you let monkeys run wild, they'll eat you out of house and home. But they're so cute, and they're so endear-ing and so . . . just like kids, you can't assassinate the kid when he pisses you off, you know [laughs]. You have to take the whole package!

So . . . that's my Yoga project . . . to see . . . where [the monkey, which he holds up] is such a fly in the ointment . . . while at the same time being one of the most endearing qualities that I am. He's the clever part of me, he's the one that's funny and fun to be with. And he's also the one who can screw things up.

To me that's my spirituality. . . . Not caving in to cultural assump-tions, but at the same time, again, not throwing the baby out with the bathwater.

KS: To acknowledge the worth and cleverness of the cultural assump-tions?
MC: Exactly, and the only way you can acknowledge their worth is to recognize that they have limitations, and the only way you can

recognize that they have limitations, is to recognize that they have worth. Because, otherwise, you pretend that the monkey is not here; you pretend that the elephant is not in the living room. Because, well that fucks everything up! [For] how can you allow for the demonic . . . for the undemocratic . . . for the unfaithful . . . for the relentless monkey mind, when those aren't our values. So we need to come back to the Buddhist sacred "middle way," [which states that] the object of our terror is also the instrument for our redemption.

We can't have it both ways. We can't have it where—"I want the redemption!" but somehow ignore the terror-inducing aspects of the potential liberation, or potential redemption.

KS: Yes, you have to have something to be redeemed from.
MC: And that goes back to the ego thing again. I really feel that our society worships the ego, and culturally we're not able to let that worship go. So we fight that sense of awe, that sense of insignificance in relation to the whole, either through materialism, scientism, or through creationism. There has to be another way. For me . . . the answer lies in going through rather than going around or vaulting over, kind of doing a spiritual detour. The spirituality . . . equips me—[with] the armor of God—to move through these challenging times, not to take away the need to move through these challenging times.

KS: Can you tell more of how you see the dimension of awe as healing for yourself and for the world?
MC: I'll give it a try. . . . In terms of my own ongoing process of recovery and also in my teaching Yoga and gymnastics, and in discussing philosophy in lecture situations, what my passion is about is to name the "elephant in the living room." And I love talking to people and saying, "You know, sometimes my monkey mind is so busy that I don't have time to listen to myself breathe. Does that ever happen to you?" And almost without exception, the whole room nods their heads. And to me, that naming and demystifying and putting "on the table" for discussion is the way of the liberation. And I use a lot of telling my own story. It's much easier to talk about my monkey

mind and how it affects me than to give you a treatise on how your monkey mind is stunting your growth [laughs]. So . . . it's like one person speaks up about his "monkey mind" and others respond, "Oh, yeah! Are you kidding? I'm TORTURED by those voices chattering in my head too; I just never heard them called 'monkey mind.'"

The idolatry of consumerism; the idolatry of one religious creed; or the plug into "one size fits all." It's like, "Oh, that's it." It [becomes] a codiscovery. And you can only discover stuff when you realize you don't know everything, and that's where awe really comes in. Once that comes in . . . then ego doesn't have such a powerful hold. It's like when you and I have discussions, we go into a different realm and in that realm we discover things. We're not teaching each other. Well, we are—but we're not instructing each other. We're going, "Ah, look at this stone that's been weathered by time and stuff, and you crack this one open and it's a geode, wow!" And that openness to discovery and surprise is a big part of what I think is going to be our salvation. . . .We have to let go of that false idol of certainty, and then look through the lens of uncertainty, of awe, and then through that lens, we'll see our salvation. And it'll look different to different people. But you have to step through the looking glass in order to get to the other side. You can't just go, "Oh, that's ridiculous, nobody can step through the looking glass . . . !"

KS: Discovery is a huge factor . . .
MC: Yes, discovery is a big part of it. It's the uncovering, the unveiling; stripping away cultural assumptions, and seeing what is, with that sense of wonder—let's do that again, a sense of astonishment in our awareness of being itself. The fact that what is, is. And I think that's the scariest, most horrific, terror-filled nightmare that we have, but also the way to our salvation.

KS: Salvation being?
MC: It's like God can't heal some sin that I've committed unless I name it, unless I open it up, I open my heart up and I'm vulnerable. And I really do think that part of the symptomatology of our empire

in decline is this inability for self-examination. But unless we do, we're absolutely flying blind, we have no bearing, we have no sense of orientation, we have no fluid center.

In summation, the sense of awe, the sense of possibility . . . is that we only touch our strength by admitting our powerlessness. And that can be really misinterpreted a lot, [such as] "being powerless is abject despair," and that kind of thing. No, it's just recognizing it. It's accepting that there are limits to our existence, and the way we overcome those limitations is to see and name those limitations, and a by-product of actually seeing what is, as it is, is that we move on. We don't get stuck.

But the whole thing about enlightenment, about illumination, is not about a fix. It's about loving what is. And from that place, then all things are possible. But if you try to force the fix, either politically or religiously or economically, you put the cart before the horse, then you never meet the horse.

KS: Back to discovery.

MS: Yes, it's that antidote to that "been there, done that" ennui, that boredom with existence . . . like Columbus saying, "I don't need to go this way, because Marco Polo's already been to India and I know all about it." And so he comes to the new world, and [he realizes] it's a new world. So we just have to open ourselves up to the fact that we don't know everything and that's not abject resignation or defeatism; it's really total realism, and then we bring to bear not only our realistic problem-solving side, but we also then bring hope and inspiration, and faith, and the promise of grace.

Like Jesus said, I come to comfort the afflicted and afflict the comfortable, and I'm not here to comfort the comfortable. [*Editorial note:* Later, following our interview, Michael equated his religiosity to a melding with ambiguity, a "religiosity of ambiguity," where one can "fall down" to drugs, food, indulgence, etc., or "fall up" to Puritanism, absolutism, fundamentalism—either way, diverting from the fundamental puzzlement of our being, and the chance for a full and dynamic life within that puzzlement. —KS]

7

AWAKENING THROUGH CHRONIC ILLNESS

How does the cultivation of awe "speak to" the chronically ill? How can a person who feels "broken" contemplate, let alone nurture, a sense of the wondrous? While there are no simple answers here, of course, our next interviewee appears to provide some radiant insights. Among these, for example, are his own hard-won efforts to "step outside the box" and cultivate an enlarged vision of both himself and his pain—not by looking past the pain, but alongside it somehow, coupled to it. These are at least a few of the gems to which we are treated.

E. Mark Stern is a remarkable man. An emeritus professor and therapist by profession, a life-philosopher by avocation, and a poet by cultivation, Mark, as he likes to be called, is a renaissance maverick. At seventy-five, Mark is a stage-three cancer survivor, but also a survivor of banality. My ties to Mark go back to our days in the governance meetings of the Division of Humanistic Psychology of the American Psychological Association. As a mentor and friend, he showed me the ropes of the deliberative proceedings, and he filled me in on the early days of humanistic psychology. As of this writing, Mark had extensive surgery for colon cancer—which followed, just a few years prior, a protracted battle with heart disease that culminated in a heart bypass procedure.

Mark knows chronic illness, and he also knows chronic vitality—he has bathed abundantly in both.

E. MARK STERN AND AWE-BASED FAITH

KS: What does the notion of awe mean to you?
MS: Expectation (as in advent/adventure); awakening (as in epiphany); communion (as in intimacy). To invoke and to allow my person (my autobiography) and all that underlies my person (known and unknown) into dialogue and participation with the wonders and tempests of existence. Awe is what Peter Berger alluded to in one of his book titles as "the sacred canopy" inclusive of individual experience even as it transcends divisions. Awe is the aesthetic of universal concern, moving, as personal experience, beyond the ties to arbitrary boundaries. Paul of Tarsus, writing to the Galatians, appears to appreciate awe-based knowledge as universal generosity: "If you are led by the Spirit, no law can touch you" (Galatians 5:18, Jerusalem Bible). And what freedom there is to act is of little comfort if that freedom be divorced from the sensibilities and interconnectedness of awe/spirit. Thus awe never suggests quiescence. As always evolving, awe mediates between distinctions even as it provides the frame of reference for an expanding communality. By the blurring of distinctions, awe moves empathy into renewed generativeness. By urging dominant species to increasingly take up the mantle of creation, awe redefines and revives the mission of humanity. Whether through globalization and/or gene and organ transfer, all are made one. Foretold by the heartbeat of creaturehood, the infinite rhythms and forms of life's diversity converge through both novelty and continuity. Self-knowledge, awe-inspired, moves into a universal sensitivity. Still, in awe, nothing is ever lost. Jorge Luis Borges reflects on awe's ultimate power of intimate redemption.

> A man sets out to draw the world. As the years go by, he peoples a space with images of provinces, kingdoms, mountains, bays, ships, islands, fishes, rooms, instruments, stars, horses, and individuals. A short time before he dies, he discovers that the patient labyrinth of lines traces the liniments of his own face.[1]

KS: What is the basis for your sense of awe?

MS: Awe is my sometime fellow-traveler. I don't feel in a position to offer concrete backing for how this all happens. At the outset, perhaps a mix of mystery and labyrinth. One ingredient I am quite certain about has been an evolving sensitivity to other(s). Say, a passion for life beyond my personal existence. This involves some visible experience. Other intuitive sensibilities, though only somewhat comprehended—say, "through a glass darkly." Sharing an uncommon soul—regarding soul as shared vagueness, yet emerging/converging as a mystical (enough) unit. Seen and unseen, "my" soul encompasses alivenesses, neighbors and strangers, events long past and others in random formation, locales both recognized and others vaguely recognized. Déjà vu; synchronistic; profane/sacred; consumed and consuming; en rapport. One person; another; incident; occasion, passing on information. Not withstanding [the authoritarian personality researcher Stanley] Milgram's observations, a sense of an underlying samaritanship. My vague experience of awe is so everyday. Other moments stand somewhat outside of time. There was the time, as a four year old, when I grabbed a toy shovel from another boy with whom I was sharing a sand pile. In all innocence, I hurled the shovel over an adjoining embankment. Suddenly, the other child's face metamorphosed. It embodied not just the pain of loss. More, his every facial muscle conveyed an embodiment of despair for who I was then *at that moment*; the hatreds I had shared for him, probably from birth. That face was to haunt me up to this very minute. And even beyond haunt, it was to transform. That boy was/is the Christ figure. Suffering not for himself, but for me. Invoking me to extend my person, my soul. Invoking me to a communion with the estranged. People, events, places (known and perhaps to be known) (lost and found, in waking and dreaming states alike). Urging me into a desire to behold (not your ordinary "seeing"). It is as if frailty, creation, and endurance had sought me and my participation. And like Jacob wrestling with the angel, to bear a new name. Mind you, I only now vaguely appreciate what that name might be. It is as if the name, once spoken, is just as soon forgotten. I live in exile from that name. And yet, it recurs. Most often, it recurs as the erstwhile lad becomes someone I have, as recently as today, belittled. I cannot run far from the disquieting vision. Though sometimes he/she/it is the joyous embodiment of my soul. A self distinct from myself, yet known to me even as the visitation happens. In words attributed to the apostle Paul: "When he shall appear, we shall be like him." A self: a lost and forgotten name is what I wrestle with; what I know to be me and what I know, as well, to be the other. The basis of awe? A confluence of tragedy and search in which "every soul is like a drop without whom the whole universe would thirst."[2]

KS: What role has awe played in recovery or healing in your life—particularly with reference to chronic illness?
MS: I have written [elsewhere] about my quadruple heart bypass . . . and the surgeon's visitation (he knew me like few others have, even if he wasn't totally aware of it). As a surgical patient, he was in my bosom and I (even under anesthesia) was radically responsive. I too played my role. Awe-fullness/being the brunt of intimidation, overwhelmed (that's awe too) and then awestruck and in harmony with him as if we were two in one. Ultimate intimacy. Much of my cure was my reparation, my animation—and with my cancer my "belly dance" in tune with my surgeon's capacity to dance in my body. I used to suggest to my students that psychotherapy is necessary in cases of receiving donated organs. One must rise to the occasion of another being accepted into the orbit and orchestration of the one with the hollowed out space needing to be filled by that other's heart, kidney, liver, blood. To be cured is generosity accepted. To be cured is linkage with all life.

As indicated earlier, life-threatening illnesses have been my fellow travelers going back to infancy and childhood. I was a severely asthmatic infant; had a compromised immune system owing to serious difficulties swallowing and digesting food and leading to childhood anorexia; at age seven I sustained a life-threatening infection of the mastoid bone (the surgical intervention doctor gave me a 30 percent chance of survival). Diverticulitis beginning as a late adolescent and young adult. Later in life, heart disease, ultimately undergoing quadruple cardiac bypass surgery. Most recently, colorectal cancer (stage-three upon nine-hour surgery). In addition to excising the cancer and two affected lymph nodes, needed corrective surgery for adhesions which had been causing increasing major abdominal pain. Adhesions caused by a "botched" appendectomy at age ten. Post-cancer surgery; chemotherapy resulting in painful and enduring neuropathy in my legs and feet. Poor balance mechanism causing me to fall when unaided by walking stick.

Awestruck far back. I was certain that I was in the company of a twin on the moon. We were in constant "contact." I have learned to appreciate this imaginal period as the manifestation of reverence for the mysteries of the spiritual cosmos. A sense of "angelic" presence permeates from childhood on. A sometime incident stands out. I was in need of a blood transfusion weeks after my mastoidectomy. The practice back in the mid-1930s was to directly transfuse from a donor. My father was my donor. I was initially fearful of the extra-thick needle required for this procedure. In the midst of my fear, a medical intern (I think he was) entered the room. His presence was beatific, eliciting from me a resonant awareness of being protected. My sense of his extraordinary proximity had a profound positive impact on me. I recall an equivalent experience about a year earlier. I was as "lost" as a continually distracted first grader could be. As a class, we were visited by a group of second graders. A boy approached my seat. His name was Christian and he was wearing a tie clasp that had in its center an image of a sailboat in peaceful seas. As he began speaking to my shyness, I experienced a healing resilience. And the summer of that same year, I was sent to Blue Mountain Summer Camp in Honesdale, Pennsylvania. My loneliness was near crippling. One night we were visited by a group of Native Americans. They did several ritual dances around a campfire. Suddenly, a beautiful young woman danced alone. I craved her comfort. And was not amazed at all that given the large crowd of campers, she chose to come to me and gently kissed me on the cheek. This too was cosmic deliverance (and much the promise of how future visitations might be expected to grace who I was, particularly during moments of greatest need). For me, the efficacy of remedies counts for less than does the simple fact that anxiety, fear, and doubt have at the most opportune moments been met by rejuvenating forces.

I can't necessarily see awe (the noun) in the same light as the verb. The verb expresses process: to be overwhelmed, impressed, moved, blown away. Awe is alive in constant process. As a reference point in my personal healing, awe was more the discoverer than the discovered. Linking links, Christian Science, which reframes illness as erroneous thinking, indeed error itself, also ministers to what illness is trying to express beyond the form it takes: Phineas Parkhurst Quimby, Mrs. Eddy's half-acknowledged inspiration for her doctrine. Philosophies prior to his own might have used terms like "soul and body" "spiritual and/vs. natural." Quimby, in fact, employs a whole other vocabulary. To the mid- to late-nineteenth-century question, "Is the person spirit or matter?" he might reply, "Neither, the person is life." And healing becomes a oneness with life, at-one-ment (as operational, but proclaiming a common identity). Deity is Infinite Mind and its Infinite manifestations. God is love, intelligence, light (why not awe?). And illness (and the basis of its "cure") both organic and functional, reflects a deep conflict between how we have customarily believed it as mere pathology *and* the wondrous struggle, vying for our limited/limiting self-concept and the mystery of awe, that is, cosmic factors. *No*, I had long, long ago erased Christian Science from my obligations. Yet, in my various latter-day brushes with life-threatening illness, some of it remained as my way of envisioning healing. A major revision from Christian Science to a "mature" view was my dedication to wanting to know what the dis-ease could (in my imagination) both symbolize and aspire to. Also in my teen years, I had read Philip Wylie's *Age of Vipers*. I recall his referring to malignancy as the will to renewing/rebuilding the body. Vision is (perhaps not) everything, but as it psychologizes the physical, it transforms illness to further engage meaning and intention.

As a psychotherapist, I have sensed the importance of casting a lasting presence on those who suffer. Bringing light into the darker caverns; presenting my being as a means of my patient's need for ablutions; and gently knowing that my most creative spontaneity becomes a means of praying *to my patient*; these are the customs which characterize my own healing place.

Before my quadruple bypass surgery, I sought the presence of my spiritual mother, Marie Nelson. On the eve of my surgery, I addressed her. "Marie," I asked, "What is it like to die?" "A cinch," she replied. This was awe. Awe was also the recovery from anesthesia. Marie "accompanied" me to my initial/diagnostic consultation with the surgeon who ultimately operated on me for colon cancer. This time around, I went into deep meditation before the doctor entered the examining room. Marie met me around a campfire (recall the summer campfire?) where she once again initiated me into her spiritual care. I was transformed by the awe, the calm elevation of my mood—the absence of all fear, and a welcoming of the surgeon "into my body." I had once again realized what Tillich refers to as "New Being," and "Spiritual Presence." That is, revelation, reunification, and reconciliation—a negation of the ego without the loss of identity.

KS: What specific role has awe played in your specialty (e.g., as educator, therapist, etc.)?
MS: Awe is, in one special sense, the excitement of participation. Translated into process, awe befriends depth psychotherapy—not by promising to remove all pain, rather by addressing (with reverence) the pained person; not by eradicating his conflict. Instead by paying attention to the role of friction and combat as the exile's resolve to cross the desert; not by encouraging the positive, more by paying attention to who one is; finally, not by dismissing sin, but more important, by seeking fellowship within the tragedy of alienation and estrangement. Shakespeare gleaned an appreciation of intimate soliloquy as silent awe and ultimate personal responsibility. Witness these lines from Macbeth:

> Doctor: Not so sick my Lord,
> As she is troubled with thick-coming fancies,
> That can keep her from rest.

Macbeth:	Cure her of that;
	Canst thou not minister to a mind diseased;
	Pluck from the memory a rooted sorrow;
	Raze out the written troubles of the brain;
	And with some sweet oblivious antidote,
	Cleanse the stuff'd bosom of that perilous stuff
	Which weighs upon the heart?
Doctor:	Therin the patient
	Must minister to himself[3]

Being alive is hardly contingent on "positive self-regard" nor on a culturally determined "happiness." Using a Tillichian analogy, self is both the actualization of Creation as it is of Adam and Eve's Fall, of good and evil, of Charles Manson and St. Francis, of despair and hope. Awe as the awakening, the quickening of destiny and option; of genetics and nurturing; of beauty and beast. Awe is wonder; advent; pleasure; pain; illumination; pitch-dark. Considering my awe: I laugh at the foibles of my past; the way my pain confirms my mortality; my sense that mystery has increasingly become my vision; multi-meanings; tears of sadness, tears of joy, tears of accomplishment, tears of loss. I have recently learned that in Hebrew, fear and faith are synonymous. I am a cobweb of fears, and my faith is unwavering. Figure? In my field? As a psychologist? A growing sense of what happens, of what matters, not only to me, but to what appears larger than "me"—super-individual is what Andras Angyal would call it. I see my vocation as developing in empathy even as I consider my earlier shame and privacy.

Now, at times, I have become like some schoolboys in Robert Frost's poem *Steeple Bush* who, simply by staring, invade the privacy and indeed sovereignty of another boy who seems "different" than them. In other words, I become an invading self. . . . Is not classification itself part of the method of science? Hippocrates separated illnesses without seeing syndromes of heaven and hell in all conditions. On the other hand, I may have outlived Hippocrates. The syndromes become more and even more mysteries; their remedies, surprises (thank you, Dr. Reik). On another note: I continue to reexamine my own past and (converging or not) the pasts of those I parent and of those I see professionally. All time is linkage in the chain of being. As I dwell on the nuances of my vocation, I know that my own healing takes on the transformative nature of practicing unity in diversity. According to the Hsinhsinming, one of the earliest treatises on Zen Buddhism notes that when activity is stopped and there is passivity, this passivity again is a state of activity. So it is with life's finished episodes. They have reigned and now they resurrect in greater fullness.[4]

Tillich's standby notion of "The Eternal Now"[5] to me represents a sense of awe (not in the waiting) but as an always opportunity of return. Return to what? Not to rule out the Thee of Augustine, "my heart will not rest until it rests in Thee oh Lord" yet more significantly, to a point (not a destination) where sensibility and a sort of "ah ha" converge. For those whose struggles with alienation are from pain, addiction, anxiety, wrath, despair, there is a sense of somewhere . . . within the fabric of experience . . . of awe as calling. The New Testament speaks to what I'm trying to say: "Come to me all you who are weary and I will give you rest." This active (like the currents in the sea) though often faint call comes in all sizes, dimensions, texts, but not again as "fixed" for a result. . . . "It is that still small voice," in and out of time (in dreams and in waking), calling for a return to sobriety, serenity, poise, healing. . . . A call infers welcome, never a spiraling toward, instead a response, even a deed or transaction of surrender, an act of bridging (bringing all that is experience with all that evokes fulfillment). The prodigal was met along the road on his way back to his father's house. Awe is assent in action. An acknowledgment that there is an "eternal" (this brings up even more than one can realize) "now" (there never has not been a *now*) re-presenting return/healing/process/potency. Awe-acknowledging therapy witnesses (through what some might term "positive transference") the drama of the call.

Awe is not a deity, yet it suggests a deified state of being, or at least, participation in a Pentecost. May I suggest awe as heightened present existing as unbound to time? Then, of course, we're into peak experience. Awe (shucks), it's more than a peak. . . . Awe is, to my mind, and in current parlance the Sabbath of ordinary experience.

8

AWAKENING IN AGING

The autumn of life brings with it the great ripening of experi-ence. Too often, especially in our Western world, we fail to appreciate this ripening and relegate our aging process to a slow slide into irrelevancy—or at best, mediocrity. Yet aging, like ill-ness, is not the one-dimensional millstone our society so often presumes. In the first part of this chapter, Christina Robertson reports on the life experience of twenty noneminent "creators" over the age of sixty-five. Although each creator (or creative individual as judged by a questionnaire) has never achieved sig-nificant fame or wealth or material acquisition, each has attained a profound sense of awe. This outlook has lifted them out of the humdrum of life—beyond their pills and palliatives—and into an extraordinary new vista. This vista explodes the myth of their decrepitude, and the quick-fix "patch-ups" so commonly—albeit tragically—pursued.

In the second part of this chapter, an Episcopal priest, Charles Gompertz, shows how a lifetime of devotion to liturgy can translate into a living devotion to Creation. For Charles, life is his ministry, and awe its guiding spirit.

REFLECTIONS OF SOME AWESTRUCK ELDERS

What follows is from Christina Robertson's (1995) landmark investigation, "Creativity and Aging: A Study of Creative Older individuals."[1] Although this research is ostensibly on creativity, the author sent me the following excerpts illustrating participants' reverence, humility, and wonder, or in short, awe—and they are well worth noting. Robertson writes:

Rebecca, a sixty-six-year-old painter, writer, musician, and former dancer, spoke of the "epiphany" [she experienced] in her first figure drawing class when she saw her first live model: "A chorus of angels sang," she said. "It was just wonderful. And I knew in that moment I would never, ever tire of the human figure—as nature's most profound and varied form. . . . And I haven't."

Barry, a sixty-seven-year-old world traveler, Internet book dealer, orchid-grower, and former teacher of world cultures, [had this to say about his about his return to his native land]: "You know, I think one of the greatest experiences of my life is coming back to Nebraska with my son. We came back and the hill cranes were migrating along the Platte River—these seven-foot-high birds. You see *thousands* of these things. I was enormously excited."

Bob, an osteologist (bone collector) and former biology teacher, remarked [about his special art]: "I got hooked on bones in art school. 'Cause bones, not just skulls, but pelvises and vertebrae and limb bones are pieces of sculpture. I refer to them as nature's masterpieces of sculpture. They're architectural wonders." When students asked him about God and religion, Bob elaborated:

I get my religion; I see my spirituality when I see the sunrise [or] a moonrise, [or] sunset. When I see an electrical storm. In wintertime, I go out to the ocean and watch the waves crashing on rocks. . . . My cathedral is the cathedral of redwood trees and I would show [students] a picture with the light, the rays of light, streaming through the trees. That's my cathedral. But I never think about God and all this stuff. My whole life is devoted to art and nature. And so I look at clouds, and the sky, and electrical storms . . . and I said, "Wow! This is it! This is my religion!"

Rebecca expanded on her sense of reverence and humility: "I feel every breath I take is a breath of thanksgiving for life in all its vicissitudes. And I not atypically spend time in the morning thinking about my day, what lies before me, and not setting specific goals but really being cognizant and making a point of being present. And then also, when I go to sleep at night, savoring the wonderful things that have taken place in the day. So I consider these a kind of reverential way of being in the world."

Sam, a seventy-three-year-old cost and manufacturing consultant, expressed his [sense] of humility when he said: "My religion provides rules for conduct. It has more to do with how man should treat man. I believe in God. I think man is too puny (which is also [the view] of the Jewish religion) to have all the answers."

Ivan, an eighty-three year-old artist and cartoonist, stated a similar belief when he noted: "I do not think we know answers. I think we have been created or manifested to live on the surface of the planet. Infinity and eternity are things we cannot fathom and I don't want to try. . . . God is so much bigger than us. . . . Whatever he is, he or she, or whatever, is so much bigger than us. How dare we think that our way is right and nobody else's way is right?"

Closely connected to "wonder," "reverence," and "humility" are the "miracles" and "mysteries" participants mentioned in connection with their creative work. Caroline, a seventy-three-year-old painter, former librarian, and community activist, was asked, "How often do your paintings turn out the way you think they will in the beginning?" She responded, saying, "I'm always amazed. It's like a miracle."

Asked where that miracle comes from, Caroline replied, "I don't know. I keep saying 'Where does this come from?' And, I guess it comes from inside. Some people, I've talked to other artists about this, some people think that it doesn't come from inside. You are just a vessel [they say], and so OK, I'm enjoying what I'm doing."

Asked whether there is any connection with spirit for her or spiritual feeling, she says, "When I said I'm an atheist, I guess I should have said I'm an agnostic because I feel as though I don't need to know. I'm just glad it comes. And maybe if I did know, it would take away from it. The mystery is nice."

When asked if she considered herself spiritual, Caroline said she "considered herself very spiritual." When a belief in something greater than the self was included, Caroline stressed her spirituality came from *within* rather than being a force outside herself.

Barry talked about how he came to enjoy a feeling of mystery through his experiences in China rather than trying to control what happened. "Well, I enjoyed everything. We went to the beach one day. And I'm not a beach person. But the Chinese are very circumspect. We left to go to the beach. Then we stopped, and we were waiting, and I said, 'What are we doing?' 'Well, two people are joining us' [was the reply]. Then we got into this taxi and we stopped. I said, 'Where are we going?' 'We're going to tea at so-and-so's house.' So we got to the beach at four o'clock. I never knew what was happening. You know? Like what was coming off. . . . But I sort of, I came to enjoy that."

Asked what it was that he specifically enjoyed, Barry replied, "Well, you don't know what's coming off so there's a sense of . . . mystery about it. But yeah, I enjoyed *everything*."

Bernard, a ninety-two-year-old poet, former engineer, and scientific writer, made a similar observation: "The greatest achievement of the human mind is the question mark."

When Rebecca was asked where her "drive to discover" comes from, she noted, "There needs to be some element there that is truly unknown and perhaps unknowable. And, I think that a very driving kind of curiosity for me is to just grapple with those kinds of issues. . . . I guess I have a large capacity for being at peace with the fact that unknowability is an essential part of life. If we knew all, why would we live? What would pull us on?"

In a similar vein, Ivan was asked about "cosmic questions," and about God, and replied, "I believe in God. I think I really do and I think it's a bigger thing than God said, 'Boom, here are people. Boom, here are fish.' Rather, a seed is planted and the seed develops on the surface of the planet."

"And God did that?" Ivan is asked. His response: "I think it's bigger than that and I don't know the answers. I don't know the answers. And I prefer not to know too much, because how much is there to know for us? We are human beings. We are not God. And I think that it is a mistake that a lot of people make [when] they think they are God or they speak for God. We're not. . . . I respect that there's something bigger than me; something more important than me."

CHARLES GOMPERTZ AND THE MINISTRY OF LIFE

Charles Gompertz is a seventy-three-year-old "priest worker" in the Episcopal church. I had the privilege of meeting Charles through Christina Robertson, the author of the study quoted from above. Although I don't know Charles in any personal sense, I feel a strong resonance with his calling. From what I can gather, he is the kind of priest (or for that matter, rabbi, minister, or "advisor") that I would feel comfortable reaching out to at times of spiritual quandary. Charles has spent his lifetime in suburban and rural places here in the San Francisco Bay area. He loves being outdoors and watching the natural world unfold around him, but even more importantly, he seems to tend to that natural world—which includes his ranch, his cattle, his olive grove, his consultation business, his family, and yes, even himself—like a minister who tends to his congregants. That is, he exhibits a zeal for living, *all* living, when it is adhered to with care. Charles strikes me as a superb exemplar of the adage "to age with grace." Accompany him now, as he lights our way along his path.

KS: What does the notion of awe mean to you?
CG: Awe is difficult to pin down. To me it means a response to an awareness of a dimension outside of myself. I am caught up in experiencing being a part of something larger than myself and larger than my previous experience. Others have described this as an "oceanic" feeling; others have said that this is an experience of love in the world. Whatever it is, it is getting outside of the usual level of experience into another dimension of reality. With this new level of awareness colors can appear brighter, sounds sweeter, light more luminous, and life somehow lifted to a different plane and improved.

It could be said that awe is a feeling, an emotional state that defies logic and reason. One feels delighted, connected, and a small part of something far larger. The feeling could be described as a profound respect for Creation and other creatures—animal, mineral, and vegetable—with whom we share this planet. It is the experience of kinship with all life and all things, being a part of the much larger picture.

There are triggers to the awe experience—some are macro, such as the Apollo picture of the blue earth hanging alone in space, or the giant trees in Muir Woods or the towering cliffs of Yosemite. It could be a sweeping vista of valleys and hills or on a micro level, a leaf or insect or flower. The light in the early morning as the sun breaks over the hills and turns the moisture in the air into a gauzy, golden veil over the trees and rocks of our own little valley. It is breathtaking and holy all at once. It is a personal response to experiencing the power of being, beauty, and a connectedness to the universe as a whole. It is very close to the experience of joy.

Awe can be triggered by the work of artists and musicians. Every year, in the spring, our little community has an art auction of work by artists who paint the "rolling hills and ranches" of our area. The farms, cows, old pickup trucks, piles of hay bales, and ancient barns and fences remind us of the beauty around us every day. We are reminded that in the ordinary there is the presence of the transcendent, there to carry us beyond the daily round of chores and cares that encircles our lives. Music, be it chamber or blues, can also carry us outside of ourselves to another place. We are stopped, awed and inspired, and moved into another realm of experience. And yet another set of triggers can be found in the world of ideas. Ideas that move us, challenge us, lift us beyond our current notion of reality into another way of thinking. These too inspire awe.

Life's events can induce a sense of awe, a sense of wonder, and an experience of working on a scale outside of the daily and ordinary. Our seven Highland cows, the ones with the long hair and bangs over their eyes, have given birth to seven calves over the past two months. To see the miracle of birth, safely transacted, resulting in a new life, is a wonderful thing. One example is the first-time mom giving over to instinct—she cleans and feeds the newborn calf, getting it on its feet as soon as possible. The baby's first steps, stumbling and unsure, gradually become more sure as the experience of walking becomes more natural. Then in a day or two, the calf is running and jumping and gamboling across the meadow to follow its mother and playing with the other calves. Watching this experience of sheer joy in living fills me with awe.

Awe is a natural response to being alive, to being aware of my surroundings and experiencing those things beyond my control and understanding. Birth, the night sky, sunrise and sunset, storm and wind, wet and dry, growth of shoots and grass—these are everyday events—and each can be a source of wonder and amazement.

KS: What is the basis for your sense of awe?
CG: Each of us creates a model of our world. There is simply too much information available to our senses to process all at once. We create a filter to help us mentally digest what is going on around us. This filter is our model of the world. It patterns our thoughts, beliefs, interpretations, and awareness of our surroundings and how they influence us. Our model of the world is our reality; it is what is real for us. This often means that alternate views are rejected, challenges ignored, and change very difficult. My model of the world includes the possibility of alternate realities—that what I perceive may not be the only set of perceptions available. I try to maintain a positive orientation, a sense of wonder and of growth. I love watching children and young animals discover their world. Learning to walk expands their world, the challenges of running and jumping open new vistas and interaction with others. It is the burgeoning of life, new and unlimited by past experiences, that is so wondrous.

To have a sense of awe is to be open to our mortality and eventual death. The medieval warning, "Vivo in momento mortis"—live in the moment of death—is still valid today. Life is now and worthwhile. Aging brings its physical challenges and frustrations. We are not as agile or strong or able to endure physical work as we were when we were younger. We can assure some of the power of our youth by working out, lifting weights, and spending time walking. These will not recapture our twenty-year-old selves, but will reduce the ravages of the years. The quality of our lives is dependent upon how much responsibility we take for diet, exercise (mental and physical), and spiritual development. Life is affirmation, a gift to be relished and enjoyed.

Remember, we always have choices. Sometimes I feel trapped in other people's decisions. Then I remember, "I can say NO!" I can choose to do nothing, or something else. I can choose to speak or be silent. I can join in or go my own way. "Should" and "ought" are words to be avoided. We do what we can and we do what we must—not what we should or ought to do.

Creation is constantly being renewed and revealed. There are long and short cycles. As we get into harmony with the created order, we find our place confirmed within it. On an east-facing deck I have marked out the two solstices and the equinox as well as a place to stand to view these events. It is very comforting to watch the sun rise over the solstice marks on the appropriate dates—to mark the sun's yearly passage back and forth across the heavens. The equinox signals the halfway points and indicates that things are as they must be. The seasons and the changes leading up to them fill me with a sense of wonder and anticipation. Even in Northern California we have seasons—warm and cold, wet and dry, growing and dying. Each of these points in the yearly cycle fills me with awe: the power in storm, wind, and warm sunshine; the wonder of spring's new grass and its death in the fall; and wind-driven rain, breezes, and lightning. Awe and wonder remind me that every day is a new adventure—opportunities with new people, events, and challenges. We are active participants in this Creation and we can take joy and experience awe as we live out our places in it.

KS: What role has awe played in recovery or healing in your life?
CG: There are victories, defeats, wounding and healing in every life. The trick becomes how to recognize and own each of them and see them as integral parts of the process of living. Our victories can be as dulling as our defeats—we can become blinded by them and fail to see the lessons learned. Recovery and healing are the processes

we use to regain stasis or equilibrium in life—that balance between order and chaos, light and dark, sickness and health. Our model of the world has much to do with how we can accept healing and health, recovery and living fully. Our sense of awe is our counterbalance to being insensitive to our world and those around us. We can become so encapsulated in our model of the world, our behavior, and our way of doing things that we are oblivious to everything and everyone else. I have been guilty of this on occasion.

After a very difficult marriage and divorce I built a cocoon for myself in which I isolated myself from everyone and everything in my life. I was caught up in a depression so deep I could barely stay awake. One day, I began to look around. I saw familiar friends who reached out to me, visited me, and included me in their lives. I began to form and nurture new relationships. I remember going on outings with my children and seeing the world through their eyes, running on the beach, making sand candles, and playing in the water. Slowly I began to shake off my cocoon and break free from the past. I experienced the awe and wonder of the natural world and the beauty and depth of relationships with others.

I discovered that spiritual truth and the path to union with the Divine both lie in service to others. I also discovered that all healing is on one level spiritual. As we wake up to service, working for others, we change, we become less fragmented and we approach wholeness. As this process unfolds it inspires a sense of awe in that it is both outside and within us at the same time. We can do very little in the way of healing and recovery by ourselves. It takes the interest, concern, and love of others to bring us out, to wake us up and encourage us to rejoin life. Many years ago I posted a quote from Tagore on my office wall. It is still there to this day. "I slept and dreamt that life was joy. I awoke and saw that life was service, I acted and behold, service was joy."

As I age I am discovering all the attendant issues of this process. I have had cancer and survived. I had pains in my joints and muscles. I grew tired more easily. I could not do hard physical work all day long as I once could. I am losing old and dear friends more often to death, and I worry about finances more and more. And yet, I am discovering that there are things I can do to reverse this process. I can watch my diet, exercise more, volunteer in the community to serve others and make younger friends. Each of these is a healing activity. Each of these redefines who I am. Each of these is a source of awe and wonder. Doing twelve pushups, eating less and enjoying it more, helping out in community projects and sharing the joy of my friends is sustaining, exciting, and yes, awe-inspiring.

There is awe in the healing and recovery process. It discovers us more than we discover it. We find it without looking for it. Our loving relationship with our partner, an intimate one, where we touch and are touched in loving and warm ways. These are healing times. We must learn to be vulnerable to reaching out and being touched in turn. We open ourselves up to another and find that we are made whole in the process. This is a miracle. This is the stuff of awe, healing, and recovery.

KS: What role has awe played in your role as priest and consultant?
CG: I am a priest-worker. This means that I am a fully ordained priest in the Episcopal church, but that I earn my living in the secular world. I exercise my ordained ministry in the context of a parish church and my secular ministry in the context of the business world. As a priest I celebrate the mass, preach sermons, teach classes, and counsel with parishioners in need. As consultant I teach management classes, facilitate meetings, plan conferences, and coach executives. Actually the two roles are more similar than one might suppose.

In the role of priest I find awe in my experience of the holy. As I lose myself in celebrating the Holy Communion or leading a prayer service I find a union with those present, a very special kind of relationship that exists only in this space and in this time. There is a kind of hush that enters the room, a stillness that fills the pauses and energizes the responses. It is a holy energy that pervades and fills the space, wrapping us all in its warmth and comfort. It is a rapt attention that takes hold of the group. This is an experience of awe.

There is a power in community. It can be confirming, healing—an encounter with the Other—an awareness that we are not alone, but are part of the whole. We are bound together in a love that heals, confirms, and enables each of us. Singing and reading in unison in church force us to breathe together, which changes our minds and gives a new awareness of who we are. I enjoy facilitating this process and sharing the power of the community as it embraces the holy.

On the consulting side it is wonderful to meet people in businesses all over the world who share the same issues of management, productivity, motivation, and communication. As people learn new skills they grow in confidence and ability. They are able to take on new challenges and embrace new opportunities in their careers. Having done this for over thirty years now I have students who have been promoted up their organizations to the very highest offices. And they remind me of what we shared along the way. This is very satisfying and awe-inspiring to know that one person has influenced and assisted another to grow and mature in his or her life.

Coaching executives is very rewarding as they bring their challenges and opportunities to each session. We examine them from several different vantage points, seeing how we can limit or expand our understanding of what is going on by looking closely at our model of the world. When the person being coached sees differently, understands what was confusing, and is able to make a decision on a course of action that will address a troubling situation—this is awe-inspiring. This is healing. This is the beginning of something new. To see what we could not see, to hear what we could not hear, and to feel what we could not feel—this is powerful. This is growth.

In my mind I do not separate my roles. In addition to priest and consultant I am also a rancher—raising cattle and growing olives. These are nurturing activities as well. Tending the adult cows and their bull, caring for the baby calves, cultivating and pruning olive trees, harvesting olives and pressing them—all are consistent with being a part of Creation and being a good steward of it. As a priest cares for the parish, the consultant cares for the corporation, the farmer cares for the trees, and the rancher cares for the cattle—it is all of one piece in my mind. I do not make divisions. We handle our cattle out of love not fear. We do not shout at them, make loud noises, or use whips and electric cattle prods. We move them with words, and gentle actions into and out of corrals and chutes. In the same way I teach corporate leaders not to shout and bully their subordinates, but listen and ask, not command and tell, to get things done. There is a peace and awe to this life, being close to the land as well as being close to people in the parish and corporate world. It is being involved in much more than a job—there is family, farm, parish, volunteer activities, and business work. They are all of a piece, not separate, not distinct, but a unity which I celebrate every day.

KS: What role do you see awe as playing in the larger scope of society?
CG: We are numbed by our culture. Loud, discordant music, incessant entertainment, iPods, video on demand—the list goes on and on. It is possible to not hear a bird sing, an insect hum, or voice of a child at play—all due to the ever-present noise. This isolates us, confines us, captures us, and keeps us from a natural harmony with living things on this planet. Our response is a sort of defensiveness, a cynicism or skeptical untrusting of every thing and every one—pessimism of belief, an isolation of self that keeps us from experiencing awe and wonder.

There is a way to overcome this, and perhaps the latest political cycle is teaching us this. The Internet can involve us as well as isolate us. It can inform and persuade and encourage as well as propagandize, intimidate, and overwhelm. We can learn to come together around positive ideas and hope and new beginnings. There is a power in ideas that can change the world and us. Plato, Augustine, Galileo, Martin Luther, and Martin Luther King brought us ideas that changed their world and helped develop ours. The power of these ideas is awe-inspiring. We are hungry for this today. We need the experience of awe to cut through the cynicism and lack of tolerance that have enveloped our world for too long.

In rediscovering awe in our society we can revisit those places that have moved people for ages: Yosemite, Muir Woods, Grand Teton, Yellowstone. There are those more recent places that touch us at very deep levels too: Gettysburg, Arlington, the Taj Mahal, the Eiffel Tower, and the Statue of Liberty. There is the sense of smallness in a great cathedral—on the pavement below a towering roof way above. This is that sense of awe of relative size that is diminished by the enormity of the building or its majestic role in our society. We need to visit these places to rekindle that sense of awe and wonder to make it once more accessible in our daily lives.

We have experienced the shattering of a world economy. We have seen fortunes wiped out overnight, great businesses diminished and gone. The power of the greed, poor management, delusion, and just plain hubris that brought this about is staggering and awe-inspiring in its own way. It is not just good that inspires awe; it can be evil as well. I am in awe of the great money managers who presided over vast corporations that are now in very deep trouble or on the brink of bankruptcy. General Motors, Citibank, Bank of America—the list goes on and on. It was not so long ago that these were the names of stability, of safety and surety. Not so today. It is with a sense of awe and foreboding that I look at our economy and try to guess where it will go next. The consequences seem vast and so beyond comprehension that I am dazed and confused by it all. Awe at the human frailty that brought this about shocks the mind.

Perhaps we are moving into a new age. Perhaps we can embrace the politics of the possible. Perhaps we can transcend our human proclivity for greed, self-promotion, and selfishness to work for the common good. Perhaps. I would stand in awe of a movement toward healing of the world economy, saving the environment, and bringing peace and prosperity to the impoverished. I do see glimmers of hope, and I am in awe of people such as the latest winner of the Nobel Peace Prize, Dr. Muhammad Yunus, and his concept of microlending as a way to battle poverty. His work in Bangladesh and other places around the world gives me hope. I am in awe of his strength, perseverance, stubbornness, and wisdom to attack the problem of poverty at its root. There is a dream that in this we can kindle our hope anew and feel a sense of awe at the outcome.

KS: How does awe contrast and compare with religion, psychotherapy, and other forms of recovery and healing in our society?
CG: Since psychotherapy is not my area of expertise I will stick to religion. Religion is many things to many people, but it is essentially

a mental map of reality—a very personal map that may in some respects be shared with others. On close examination many of these mental maps are very personal and often do not closely correspond to "orthodoxy" or the creeds of an organized sect, cult, or religious organization. In other words, all Roman Catholics do not believe the same thing, nor do most Episcopalians or Buddhists or Moslems. Your belief is whatever you say it is and can convince others to follow.

Religion takes many forms. These can be categorized into: world affirming versus world denying, intellectual versus ecstatic, nurture versus salvation oriented—and on and on. Awe is the reflection of one's total response to living one's mental map. In some traditions, "accepting Jesus" is an awe-inspiring event, as is "being one" with God, or Nirvana, or attaining paradise—each describes that moment of transcendence in which the human experience melded with the Divine. The response to this is awe.

Religion is often focused on developing a capacity for awe. Learning to see, hear, touch, taste, and feel the infinite in everyday experience. The goal in Western religions is to be connected to, not alienated from, the Divine, the source of Creation, life, love, and being. In some Eastern religions the goal is to be disconnected from daily life and achieve mindlessness. Whatever works. Awe is a good connecting point as it is common to all, and yet the specific manifestation is very unique. In some religious communities shouting and exclamations of joy at connecting with the Divine is appropriate, in others it is a deep silence with the sense of awe quietly manifested within the believer.

For me, in my search for an experience of the Divine, I find that being with others is important. Christian worship as practiced in the Episcopal church with its emphasis on the Eucharist and the Book of Common Prayer I find very moving. Being in a great cathedral or a small mission church, using the same words in each place makes the moment transcendent. Chanting the service in a stone chapel or reading it in a home, each has its elegance and numinous quality. When I am alone in the fields or tending my olive trees it is often the words of the service or scripture that come to me to describe and capture the moment, filling me with awe and helping me to experience more deeply my world and my place in it.

I have a neighbor who has a sign on her road which reads, "The Journey is the Destination." This is a good description of the religious life. It is a process. It is neither consistent nor ordinary. It is a journey of discovery in which what is discovered is yourself and your relationship to everything and everyone else. Work and service to others are key elements in this discovery process. As we work we learn our limits and capacities, as we serve others we learn to go beyond those limits and capacities and create something new and often wonderful. Working with others amplifies and magnifies our abilities and contributions. Together we make something that none of us could do alone. I worked with a group of teenaged boys last spring to build a bridge across our creek. We toiled all day and with great effort moved rocks, made gravel, created footings, and built the bridge. Many tasks happened all at once. When the last nail had been driven and the last rock pushed into place one of the boys, standing uphill from the bridge, said in a quiet voice, "It is awesome." And it was. Everyone had to run up the hill to see what he saw. And it was awesome. Since it was a church group we offered prayer to bless the bridge and all the work that went into it. That was a transcendent moment, as holy as any moment in any church anywhere in the world.

9

AWAKENING
THROUGH HUMOR

One can't speak of "awe-based awakening" and forget humor. The "cosmic joke," as it has so often been called, is the realization, not just of the absurdity of our condition, but of the *wonderment* of our condition. If looked at generously, wonderment is the flip side of absurdity, just as curiosity is the flip side of stupefaction. We can languish in despair or sanctify the moment; numb ourselves with palliatives, or charge ourselves with amazement. In short, the choice is ours—awe-based *response* or despair-based reaction to the nonsensical? In the vignette to follow, comedy writer Jeff Schneider animates—and fairly detonates—awe-based responsiveness. This will be the only section of the book that trumpets the likes of Reggie Jackson's "tape-measure job" at the 1971 Major League All-Star game, or Phil Woods's recording of "Cheek to Cheek," but that is precisely why (among other reasons that will become evident) I include it. In his own inimitable style, Jeff shakes us out of our easy chairs, and calls us to life's spontaneous treasures—are we going to savor these treasures, he challenges? Or are we going to shrink back into the marrow-sapping banalities—or worse yet, barbarities, of the jigsaw puzzle life?

Note to readers: This chapter is not for the fainthearted. While it may offend some, it will move and delight others; and while it may sting, it will also stir. As Jeff notes in his opening remarks, he is not an academic but brings an "assembly-line worker's perspective" to the topic. Too often, particularly in academia, I think we neglect this assembly-line worker's view, and as a result, lose our wider message. What is that message? That awe is free, natural, and universally available—even to "pasty-faced" white guys.

JEFF SCHNEIDER AND THE COMIC'S SENSE OF AWE: WHY I LIVE

For those of you who have attempted to pierce the natural casing of my being by painting me as a horrific misanthrope, a curmudgeonly, cynical, nit-picking moaner and a dyspeptic agent of the highest order, all I can say is, "F*&% you!" You wouldn't know how to live if you had a coupon for a free week on Porn Island . . . you sorry blue-pill-popping bastard! I'm going to like bitch slap you like a fly in January if I ever see you strutting your sorry shit again. Like you got it going on, flip-flopped and tan; ready for your close-up. . . . Put the coffee down! Coffee's for closers!

I tell this story as only a layman can. I am not bogged down with academic dogma like so many professional thinkers, but bring to the problem an assembly-line worker's perspective, a football tackle's doggedness to the rigors of living in a system where true passion is ceremoniously subjugated and smashed. We live in a time of reconstitution, where a culture would rather go to the cane than let passion flow unencumbered. Freethinking has gone the way of the mumps. Dogma is the coin of the realm, and creativity has been sentenced to the clock tower. As citizens in a culture nothing is more rewarded with "pat on the head" approval than rugged capitulation. I call it this because most citizens will defend with Shiite fanaticism their roles as actors in the culture. As citizen/actors in a capitalist system we are given no choice but to "enjoy" our lives and revel in the construct that is our role. To dismiss our role is to admit that our lives might be a sham, and who could do that after living so "long and fruitful" a life?

For most people modern life is akin to living on an ant farm. You can watch this scenario during rush hour as the ants queue up on their way to the rock pile. Walk around town on any given day and talk to the people who tend to our laundry or fix our cars. Ask them to opine about the exigencies of daily life, and you'll invariably get treated to a dull stream of monosyllabic claptrap. "How's it going?" "It's going. . . ." Where's the juice? Where's the exhilaration? For most of us life has been reduced to the consistency of lukewarm gruel. Is it in us to rise above our stewardship of the mundane, our fanatic attachment to that ratty, dirty blanket? No, I don't want to go to Applebee's or meet you at the parade.

Why is it so hard for me to take succor from modern life's seemingly simplest pleasures like "American Idol" and Brangelina ("Brangelina"—in the current cult of personality—is a hybrid code for the merger of two popular entertainers: Brad Pitt and Angelina Jolie). Why is it impossible for me to understand the subtleties of standing almost nude in subzero temperatures painted in the complimentary colors of a local sports team?

I knew I was in big trouble when I saw the first Star Wars movie in 1977 and couldn't figure out what all the hubbub was about. The crowd had embraced in my view a perfunctory little science fiction film and blown it up to deific proportions. I couldn't believe or understand it. It was then as I walked out of the theater that I knew what my destiny would be and I would play that role for the next thirty years: a man with little interest in anything culture has to offer, who does not participate in any communal surface activities, who possesses no indigenous spirit toward holidays or publicly endorsed celebrations, who shuns everything remotely organized, who shrinks from his vomit-inducing role as citizen; and yet a man who will content himself to tread in the dark murk while secretly thrilling to its absurdity.

What is the genesis of this disgust? What makes this salty dog shrink in horror at the prospect of canoodling with even one morsel of sanctioned trumpery? Had our man's sense of self-worth been systematically shanghaied by the vacuity of consumer culture?

If you ever see a doughy, pasty-faced white man in his early dot-age cold-cocking mall shoppers with socks filled with horse manure dawdle a few moments while the lactic acid builds up in his tiring, yellowing extremities, he will only be too glad to meet you at the Cinnabon and repeat the process.

Why has the insignificant become so significant? Chitchat has supplanted discourse, impalement has overtaken lovemaking, commerce has become the new modern art. We look to the leaders of our times for guidance only to see them break wind and be gone. We have no problem in transferring our individuality to these keepers of the beacon, but want nothing to do with the consequences. We claim to want to know the meaning of life, yet continually spend our days denying it, pissing away our time in what Ian Anderson of the band Jethro Tull refers to in the band's masterwork "Thick as a Brick" as our "animal games."

So, if I get such little pleasure in the construct that is modern life, why do I live at all? What propels me to tie my shoes and walk out the door knowing all too well that a succubus waits behind the nearest billboard to sap me like a young maple? How does a man who hates most marketable undertakings manage to keep from inhaling deeply from a gaseous oven? Well, if you've ever been alive then you most certainly know that the vagary of existence is the spice that flavors all, a condiment so pungent and aromatic that to leave it out of the bouillabaisse of life only leads to the castration of experience and an appearance on *The Price is Right*!

Let me ask you a question. Have you ever listened to a piece of music that was so amazing that it moved you to tears? The experience was so powerful that language could not possibly describe your reaction to it. Like maybe seeing a great ball player launch himself high above the fence, flicking his glove at the last possible second, dashing the dreams of the opposing rabble. How could he do that? There was no way, and yet . . .

Perhaps it was seeing Van Gogh's *Sunflowers* for the first time, his tragic humanness emanating from each brushstroke, that became your causa sui, or seeing a love's naked body for the first time that catapulted you into a new dimension. I hate to be a killjoy, but that's it folks. That's the meaning of life. No more, no less. Each disease we find a cure for, each new planet we discover, each new symphony we compose is our way of trying to get to the ungettable, our Sisyphean mission. That's the beauty of this remorseless life. We achieve apotheosis by the mere fact that we believe we can. Greatness out of delusion.

In everyone's life there are experiences that are indelibly etched into their memory. These experiences are the closest they'll ever come to finding any real meaning in life. They are perhaps illusions, but it is because of our humanity that we inculcate them with so much importance. It is the best we can do. It is the tragedy and triumph of the human. I say fuggeddaboutit and enjoy.

For better or ill, here's my list of indelible memories—and the closest I've come to awe.

The List

1. "Cheek to Cheek" Phil Woods—Live at the Showboat—Bebop's great virtuoso cooking on all burners. One of the great arrangements in jazz history.
2. The final movement of "Close to the Edge" by Yes; it was a seminal moment in my development. Big and fulla shit, but put me at nineteen knee-deep in possibility.
3. Edda Dell'Orso's soaring wordless vocals in Ennio Morricone's undisputed and still single greatest title theme ever composed from the film *Once Upon a Time in the West*. The melody is as haunting and realized as art can be.
4. "You Make Me Feel So Young," Frank [Sinatra]—Live at the Sands. Composed by the great Count Basie; a greater, more buoyant love song was never sung.
5. Roy Hobb's titanic blast at the end of *The Natural*. A goo-ily magnificent schmaltz fest. Watch it with your kid before it's too late and he becomes a Broadway dancer. Thoroughly American, a great guilty pleasure all the way.
6. Little Olek—standing neck deep in the human detritus in *Schindler's List*, a beam of light coming through the wooden portal onto his frightened face. As I'm not normally a fan of Mr. Spielberg I give him props for his bringing the Holocaust to the masses. The image of this little boy trying to find a hiding place when the Nazis are liquidating the ghetto is one of the great set pieces in cinematic history. Beautifully rendered. Janusz Kaminski's haunting cinematography reaches an apogee here.

7. #32 Jim Brown. The Paul Bunyan of running backs. He was so huge and revolutionary for his time that he still casts the biggest shadow. The only back that any and all are always compared to. The greatest ever.

8. #23 Michael Jordan—the single greatest athlete for sheer ability, will, and fortitude to ever play. What can you say about His Airness. When he goes into the hall they need to build him his own wing—anything less is an abomination.

9. 19.32—Michael Johnson's world record in the 200 meters at the Atlanta Olympics. I watched it live and witnessed the culmination of athletic perfection. Frankie Fredericks, the Namibian sprinter who was not too shabby himself, had the lead on the stagger until Michael Johnson hit the curve and blew Frankie's doors off, producing a record that might stand for the next forty years. It still makes me shudder at the power of this magnificent athlete.

10. 43.18—ditto Michael Johnson's 400-meter world record. Not as completely dominant as the 200, but no other sprinter has ever held these two distance world records simultaneously. I might be waxing a little too much, but it is probably the greatest combined achievement in the history of track and field.

11. Reggie Jackson's tape-measure job in the 1971 All-Star game at Tiger Stadium. My memory is of watching it with my dad. When Reggie connected and it hit off the light tower in right field, my dad and I just looked at each other, our mouths agape.

12. *Denial of Death* by Ernest Becker. I was given this book by my cousin [the author of this book!] who warned me that if I read it I "would be playing with dynamite." Needless to say it destroyed my life, and I am in the process of suing the pants off him for the desecration of my hero system. One of the great books of the twentieth century. A primer gazing into the psyche and wholesale destruction of human beings by human beings. Brilliant, concise yet defiantly hopeful.

13. Patty LaBelle—"The House That I Live In." About fourteen years ago I was watching Frank Sinatra's eightieth birthday

special on the tube. A variety of A, B, and C list stars joined Frank and his wife, Barbara, to celebrate the chairman's milestone. Springsteen, Dylan, Hootie sans Blowfish curried Frank's favor with meager renditions of famous Frank tunes. It wasn't until Patti LaBelle came out and did a rendition of this overly sentimental little number entitled "The House That I Live In," a paean to patriotism and small-town community, that art decided to kick some ass. Frank had won an Academy Award for a short film he made in 1945 where he sang a very straightforward version of this song. Patti LaBelle comes out and proceeds to bust a move and pile drive the audience with an arrangement and voice so powerful that to describe it with language would be a disservice to the artistry. She infused this ham and egger with such ferocity and love that it almost became unlistenable. Her command of the material and assurance as a performer laid waste to the rest of the hackneyed entertainers who preceded her. I have it on tape and play it from time to time and am still amazed.

14. Bob Beaman's 29' 2¼" leap at the 1968 Mexico City Olympics. He broke the record by almost two feet. Beaman collapsed when he saw the length of his jump, his head in hands, overwhelmed by what he had just done.

15. Yosemite National park. El Capitan, Half Dome, Glacier Point. Nature's great salve.

16. *Thick as a Brick.* Jethro Tull's great masterwork. I was too young to understand it when I was nineteen, but thirty-three years later it still resonates with a rounded understanding of man's self-deluded dispensation for defiling everything he touches.

17. Woody Allen's *The Nightclub Years.* A great glance into the heyday of nightclub performance. Fresh as a daisy forty years later. Modern, trenchant, and still vital.

18. Valerie Brumel—The Great Russian. The Michael Jordan of the high jump. He was jumping 7' 5½" in 1962 using the western roll. Forty-three years later the record is just a little over 8 feet.

19. Bertman's stadium mustard—The China White of mustard.

20. "My Favorite Things"—John Coltrane. The National Anthem of jazz. To take a song so ponderously saccharine and transform it into a gorgeous hypnotic tribute to what is great about life is music's highest calling.

21. Dave Waddle at the tape. 1972 Munich games 800 meter final. Skinny, improbable Dave in his golf cap lunging at the wire to immortality.

22. Sammy Davis Jr. Everything Frank was and more. He lived and performed through segregation and in the shadow of F.S. Amazingly versatile and a much more talented, well-rounded performer than Sinatra. I know it sounds corny; just check him out.

23. *Manufacturing Consent*—Noam Chomsky's dithyramb about how public consent is manufactured by corporations who own and control the media outlets. A brilliant but ultimately sad treatise of our times.

24. *On a Life Well Spent*, Cicero—The antiquities had the same problems as modernity. We put our pants on every morning and go out and look for meaning. Cicero's essays about aging are as sober, sharp, and life-affirming as they come. Beautifully rendered by a man who was not afraid to enjoy!

25. *Letters to a Young Poet*, Ranier Maria Rilke—What can you say about someone so immersed in being an artist that the mere mention of commerce causes him to run for a bucket. As pure as it gets with regard to artistic calling. The unfettered commercial world could do worse than nurturing more minds like Rilke's.

26. Jock Sturges—This is an artist who has been photographing naturist families, sons, daughters, moms, dads some of them for over twenty-five years with their explicit consent, yet some still deem him a pedophile. The work done over many years captures the glories and ravages of time relating to physical maturation. Young boys and girls bloom into men and women with the forthrightness of everything great about being alive.

27. Jan Saudek—This artist from the Czech Republic suffered the slings and arrows of outrageous fortune by the hands of the Communist government for many, many years. Film was scarce. Bad jobs were plentiful, yet Saudek carried on with unflinching purpose. His work is imbued with a multifaceted humanness rarely seen today. Check out "The Love." 'Nough said.

28. Caroline—Sitting through a rancid high school production of *West Side Story* only to be saved by the beautiful voice of your own daughter.

29. Lewis—as a witness to his birth. He appeared out of the void. I was knee deep in placenta and shit, yet stood there in complete wonderment.

30. "The Vital Lie" [a chapter in Ernest Becker's *Denial of Death*]—Genius at its most trenchant. What *is* the best foolishness to live under? 'Nough said.

Final Thoughts

La Cosa Nostra, this thing of ours called Life, was as infinitesimally likely to occur as the Cubs winning the World Series. For the right chemistry to create life, the odds were so great and impossible that to take it for granted is tantamount to abdicating all that is awesome in the universe, yet we treat it like the disposable seed of youth. The human being needs to step up and realize that we are all bozos on this bus, that no one has any purchase on the ultimate meaning of life. To do this we must remove the commercial God from the equation. Only then can the person place himself in his proper place as one tiny cog in this ever-spinning, churning, roiling petri dish and not as the arrogant zenith of evolution. This will allow the person to become his own God, a god all people can aspire to.

Art and human creativity are the highest and the only callings. Artists create art because it is the only reasonable alternative to an unreasonable situation. The artist longs to get to the godhead, but knows it is impossible. The sense the artist takes from this may be paltry, but it sure beats sitting on the couch watching TV for fifty years, only getting up on Sunday to fill a destiny as a munificent supplicant.

If Rembrandt were alive today would he still have painted *Aristotle Contemplating the Bust of Homer*, or contemplating the bust of Jayne Mansfield?

III

TOWARD AN
AWE-BASED WORLD
AWAKENING:
GUIDEPOSTS TO
AN AWE-BASED LIFE

What then have we learned from our awe-informed contributors? What are their "take-home" messages and how do these
apply to our everyday lives? These are the questions to which I will
now turn, supplementing my reflection with both anecdote and art.

First and foremost I believe we have learned about *presence*—the
ability to "stay with" and closely attend to life's unfolding story.
Long the province of meditative and therapeutic practices, presence
opens the door to an expanded identity; the more that one can be
present, the more one can both acknowledge and yet move beyond
disabling fixations—the more one can open to awe. Consider, for
example, how presence to nature helped Jim Hernandez to move beyond his macho-centered culture; or how attention to spiritual questions aided Michael Cooper to break through his drug addiction; or
how attunement to marine life assisted Fraser Pierson to rejuvenate
her childhood, and so on. To sum: consider how presence enabled
our contributors to see beyond the constraints of family and culture
to a more invigorating sweep of life.

Second and directly emanating from presence, we have learned about *freedom*—or the capacity to choose, access, and deepen presence. Consider, for example, the variety of contributors who chose to be present under the most trying circumstances, such as illness, fear, and compulsion; these participants were stunned—and yet able to step back, pause, and reassess their circumstances anew.

One of the most archetypal examples of freedom—and the *courage* to exercise it—is Viktor Frankl's classic study of life in a concentration camp. Frankl shows that if human beings can find meaning—awe even—in a death camp, then they can find it most anywhere; as our contributors show too, *awe is available to all.*

Witness the following from Frankl's journal notes about a train ride between slaughtering fields:

> If someone had seen our faces on the journey from Auschwitz to a Bavarian camp as we beheld the mountains of Salzburg with their summits glowing in the sunset, through the little barred windows of the prison carriage, he would never have believed that those were the faces of men who had given up the hope of life and liberty. Despite this factor—or maybe because of it—we were carried away by nature's beauty, which we had missed for so long.[1]

In another place, Frankl wrote, "In a last violent protest against the hopelessness of imminent death, I sensed my spirit piercing through the enveloping gloom. I felt it transcend that hopeless, meaningless world, and from somewhere I heard a victorious 'yes.' . . . At that moment a light was lit in a distant farmhouse . . . as if painted there, in the midst of the miserable grey of a dawning morning in Bavaria."[2] Finally, consider Frankl's remarkable statement: "As the inner life of the prisoner tended to become more intense, he also experienced the beauty of art and nature as never before."[3]

As this last statement attests, we must add one more dimension to our essential discoveries about awe—not only does it require presence, freedom, and courage, it also necessitates *appreciation.* One could say, in other words, that in order to experience life's majesty, one needs to appreciate its fragility, and that the two comprise its vitality. This is more than just "tolerance for contrasts and contradictions," but the capacity to be moved by contrasts and contradictions, the capacity to focus on and appreciate the opportunities they present. Jim Hernandez, for example, acquired this appreciation when, as a young child, he witnessed the homeless man in the street, and later, of course, the poignancy of his many losses; Michael Cooper understood it when, following his mother's suicide, he turned to spirituality; Mark Stern experienced it when, in the throes of his illness, he connected with a compassionate surgeon; and even comedic contributor Jeff Schneider apprehended it while presiding "knee deep" at his child's birth.

Yet in spite of, and perhaps in light of, all these testimonies, the question nevertheless remains: How can the typical person—or "man (woman) in the street," realize the benefits of awe? How can such a person cultivate presence, freedom, courage, and appreciation? These are the challenges that we will now consider in some depth.

10

AWE-WAKENING
IN THE EVERYDAY

The first thing that is imperative to understand about the everyday discovery of awe is that it is also a *rediscovery*. There is no awe that has not had its correlate in one's personal or collective past. This contention is critical because it means that one does not have to "reinvent the wheel" as it were, or derive from a particular background in order to experience awe. Rather, the experience of awe permeates life. It is there in our emergence into the world, our play, and our dreams; it is present in our religions, literature, and art; and it is detectable in our primal contact with nature, as well as in our first questions about nature.

The upshot of this realization is that we are bathed in awe-based possibilities; if only we could but recognize them. Yet many of us fail to consider, let alone recognize, fundamental awe; despite its availability in death camps and suffering as we have witnessed in this book, it somehow manages to elude many of us in our day-to-day lives. It somehow gets shuttered away, compartmentalized, or forgotten; it becomes a relic of childhood, a reverie, or a special event. Yet if there is one point to drive home in this book, the offerings of awe are so much greater than most of us conceive—they are right here, right now.

CRACKING THE COSMOSPHERE[1]

About three years ago, a prominent psychologist, Howard Gardner, arrived at a very perplexing conclusion. He said that according to the latest brain research, existential intelligence, or the proclivity to ponder the "big questions" of life (e.g., why we live, what life is about), is not quite a "full-blown" intelligence. He goes on: "My hesitation in declaring a full-blown existential intelligence comes from the dearth, so far, of evidence that parts of the brain are concerned with these deep issues of existence."[2]

Now, aside from the presumption implied, this is a bewildering contention indeed. Does it really take measurable patterns in the brain to confirm what many of us sense intuitively—that opening to the enormity of life is legitimately intelligent? What other categories of intelligence are more essential? The ability to sell real estate? Or to make war? Or to design automobiles? To be sure, these and other intelligences have their place—indeed, they help to run our world; but to what extent do they lift and enrich us? How much do they move us or ignite our imaginations—or generate the creativity that fulfills our lives?

As this volume shows, we need a new priority if we are ever to overcome the collective myopia that plagues contemporary existence. We need a priority on the largeness of our lives—the largeness of life—if we are ever to dig out from under its conditioned mundanity.

To reinstate awe in our lives we need to crack open what I have coined the cosmosphere or big picture of life. We need to realize that at any moment we can peer into a breathtaking scope of reality, which can reform and replenish us. While there are many ways to enter this revitalizing domain, as we have seen, let us now consider one of the most challenging—routine living.

DAILY PORTALS AND THE LENSES OF AWE

It is one thing to seek out awe-inspiring experiences, such as by climbing mountains, gazing at statues, or journeying to exotic lands.

However, it is quite another proposition to enter the awesomeness just beneath our feet or above our heads—such as on our drive to work, or in the midst of a conversation, or even on our jaunt to the garbage can. These are the daily bits of awe, the portals, as we might call them that can revive our worlds.

While these portals can be accessed virtually anywhere, at any time, they cannot generally be approached directly. If you "look" for awe, you're probably not going to find it (or you will find a desiccated version of it); on the other hand, if you can be *open* to awe, if you can be comparatively present, free, courageous, and appreciative in your approach, then you are in more of a position to be grasped by it, and to savor its intensity. While I cannot plot out a formula for this result, I can, based on our testimonies, suggest an aid or "lens" through which awe is likely to awaken. Again, such a lens cannot "produce" awe, but it can "prime the pump," as it were, for an awe-inspired transformation. Consider, for example, "trying on" the following:

The Lens of Transience

This lens focuses on the passing nature of life and is one of our most potent contexts for awe. Although our contributors—as well as Frankl's death camp experience—put the exclamation point on this lens, there is an abundant need for many of the rest of us to simply heed its power. What I mean by this is that one doesn't have to be on a transport train from Auschwitz, or to have stage-three cancer to recognize the poignancy of passing life. One doesn't need to come face-to-face with annihilation to see that all about us annihilation is in process, and that this very fact accentuates the defiance of annihilation. Hence, to the degree we are aware, we can apprehend the stench (as well as poignancy) of dwindling time, and this alone can move us toward greater presence, freedom, courage, and appreciation. This alone can apprise us of life's gift.

That said, however, there is another form of annihilation that is even closer to our beings that is all too overlooked, and that is our own annihilation, our own *dying*. The fact is we really don't have to look far to realize that we are all in some sense receding: our ideas become outmoded, our memories fade, and our bodies shrivel. We slip, as it were, turn by turn into the great shadows of creation. Hence, if I'm walking to my bedroom at night, or putting on my clothes, or talking with my wife, I try to realize that I have an *opportunity*—a one-of-a-kind, never-likely-to-be-replicated possibility, to really take in this moment, to absorb this flicker into the blackness. I try to look at and feel the background of dwindling time, not as a press to rush, but as a reminder to attend and to savor. For again, the awe is not *in* the definable event—whether that's walking to my bedroom or putting on my clothes or even talking with my wife—it is in the implications of that event for the ongoing puzzlement that upholds and subsumes it. It is in that "foreign country" as Shakespeare put it in *Hamlet*, within which time and death dwell, and through which our living moments radiate.

Virginia Woolf had a particular way with the lens of transience. In novels such as *To the Lighthouse*,[3] she brought the cosomosphere front and center into the details of everyday life. In the opening sequence of *To the Lighthouse*, we are introduced to a collection of characters who mother, who brood, who paint, and who chastise. They are all gathered at the seaside home of Mrs. Ramsay and her family, and they all go busily about their lives. Yet all the while, the specter of time—indeed, death—is looming; few notice, but the author tracks it palpably. The house is decaying, the children are growing (as well as dying), and the sea is consuming. The specter of time becomes increasingly evident to Mrs. Ramsay because she feels it with her children—in the joy of their play, the heartache of their hurts, and the growing, acute sense that all will fade. The backdrop of death and time is also captured in Mrs. Ramsay's lonely but dynamic artist friend, Lily Brisco. As if to seize upon the last, fleeting moments before they dissolve, she presses her brush to canvas with the fury of a pent-up colt. The others in the story are significantly less aware: the husband caught in his regrets, the young student in his brashness, and so on. Yet all is against the backdrop of erosion and change, darkening and obscurity. At the end of the story, Mrs. Ramsay dies and the remaining family returns ten years later for a visit. The house is a pale imitation of what it once was, and the sands have eroded the property. Yet out of these ravages comes a renewed appreciation, not only for Mrs. Ramsay, but for the life she radiated.

I sometimes experience a parallel sensation when gathering at the ocean with my son and friend. As I am able, I open to our movements—or stirrings, as Jim Hernandez put it—of play at sea. I become acutely aware of the beat of the sun on our welcoming shoulders, the refreshing spray of waves, and the expressions of delight on our collective faces. As we play, I grow increasingly conscious of the brevity of these exuberant moments—particularly in the context of my son. I feel the twinge of poignancy against this background, and the deepening of all we feel and do. Not to say that I become fixated on this background, just aware, and for me, this awareness charges our entire experience.

The point here is not to indulge in the lens of transience, but to peer into it, see how it affects one, and take in the sensations that it arouses. Further, the lens of transience may not be for everyone; young people for example, may not have the background (or inclination) to appreciate it. Yet I am convinced that for many, at many points of living, the awareness of the passing nature of time can be profound, if not life-turning. Not only does it move one concertedly in the direction of the cosmosphere, it extends and accentuates that sensibility, wherever and whenever one accesses it.

The Lens of Unknowing

Following quickly on the heels of transience is unknowing—or the realm of the unknown. Unlike transience, which focuses solely on time, the unknown extends to all dimensions—time, space, mind, and heart. Unknowing eclipses all and tantalizes us with the source of all. It is the "worm at the core" but also the dazzle, grace, and hope at the core. Although the unknown may be the strongest factor in the kindling of fear, as Rod Serling, the creator of *Twilight Zone* intimated,[4] it also may be the strongest factor in the fostering of fascination. Consider for example, the role of unknowing in film, literature, and fine art. How mesmerized we are by suspense thrillers, tales of adventure, and enigmatic characters. How we stammer before sculpture, painting, and hymnals. Indeed, the whole of our natural world is a wonder, riddled with obscurities, both large and small. Scientists such as Einstein stand rapt before this spectacle, and fill with exhilarating curiosity. But so do—and can—many of us the moment we stop to reflect.

The unknown explains the lure of the hunt, the search, and the risk—and not just in movie houses or forests, but in problem-solving, conversing, performing, playing, lovemaking, traveling, and craftsmanship. It lends to life the quality of a journey and all the thrill, chill, and anticipation thereunto associated. Although we are rarely aware of it, we venture into the unknown every time we step out of—or into—bed, every time we eat, drink, or breathe. Indeed, we are suspended in the unknown, despite every effort we make to blunt and defy it.

Did you ever consider, for example, the enigma of a face? Did you ever look closely at the eyes or stand back and absorb the outlines of the nose and mouth; or the tilt of the head and arch of the eyebrow? Or the way a smile lights up a room, or a look could "kill"? This is not the way most of us are accustomed to observing, and yet if we did, more of us might perceive like artists—with repeated wonder. We might persistently be filled with curiosity, for example, or marvel at subtleties. How could looks kill, we might ponder, or light up a room? Where do all these expressions come from and how do they seize us? "The unknown wears your face," Dr. Jekyll informs his girlfriend, Muriel (in the film version of *Jekyll and Hyde*), "and it looks back at me with your eyes."[5]

Who are we, what are we, and where are we headed? These are not just abstract musings or the by-products of idle minds; they are sensibilities that form attitudes that can invigorate life. I once had a therapy client who had bouts of depression but who could shift those bouts the moment she adopted the lens of unknowing or "bird's-eye view." She would be driving to my office in a funk, but then she would notice the trees bending in the wind or the flowers dotting the roadside. She would look at the people scrambling all about—like ants—and wonder what it was all for. Then she would turn to herself and her own accustomed habits (which included fears, sorrows, and frustrations) and she'd begin to wonder what they were really all about. Then she'd begin to laugh as she considered all the wondrous and absurd lives we lead, filling some unknown role, dissolving into some unknown mist. Now, to be sure, not everyone can see through to this wide-angle view, but with a little encouragement many people could perhaps expand the angle through which they are accustomed to approaching the world.

In the end, unknowing fosters transcendence of fixation: the eclipsing of gloom and the lifting of sorrow, the enlarging of admiration, and the balancing of despair. To the extent that we can perceive failure or rejection or fate, not as end points but way stations in the grand sweep of creation, we are on our way to wizened unknowing.

But besides bringing a healing element to experience, unknowing also brings an educative element as well. When my son was a toddler, I would take him outside, pick him up, and show him the stars. I would often talk with him about these marvels, and wonder with him about where they came from and who or what may occupy them. The capacity to appreciate mystery, as Rollo May too had so eloquently intimated in the opening quote of this book,[6] is a critical condition for thinking let alone creativity and imagination. What we open when we open to the unfathomable is a treasure trove of hunches, questions, and ideas. Some are well-formed and some are will-o'-the-wisp, but the upshot is that they spark our capacity for discovery. They start the wheels turning, and set our sights on alternative ways to think, feel, and understand. In short, the lens of unknowing is a catalyst; it can lift us from pain, and it can rouse us from complacency.

The Lens of Surprise

A chief component of unknowing is surprise. To the extent one can open to surprise one can also enable spontaneity, novelty, and reform. Being open to surprises means being open to one's memories, dreams, and past, as well as future possibilities. One can experience this openness while sitting in one's easy chair or while driving to work. It can also occur on a walk.

The other day I was walking around my neighborhood and spotted a tractor at a construction site. As I approached the vehicle, I didn't think much about it, but as I got closer, I started to notice its smell. It was the smell of axle grease, which suddenly broke open a flood of childhood memories. The main memory was of playing amid tall grasses and scattered debris in an empty lot. It was summer, and the full complement of smells, sights, and sounds filled the air. The lot was obviously a construction site, but to me, it was a magical playland. Scene after scene flashed through my mind: climbing on wood beams, imbibing the warm dandelion-filled breezes, and most exhilarating of all, fixating on a magnificent yellow tractor. This tractor seemed immense to me as I surveyed its massive chassis. Its hydraulic arms were Herculean, and its frame, like a mastodon. I then recalled climbing on the tractor and reaching its throne-like seat. I felt on top of the world on that seat, and when I was set in position I even took a chance and fiddled with the defunct controls. I felt safe while doing this—and yet delightfully apprehensive at the same time. I also focused on the tractor's vibrant, radiating color, that bright mustard yellow that matched the sun. There was something about that color that filled me with excitement and wonder, and that tantalized me for months.

Staying open to the people we might meet or the conversations we might entertain can also bring awe-inspiring intensity. One never knows, especially if one stays amenable, whom one may connect with along one's daily path, or where such a connection may lead.

I find this potentiality to be especially notable at social gatherings where, despite preconceptions to the contrary, I suddenly find myself in a new level of dialogue with a person; and more often than not, it is a person I least expected to engage. I learn new things about myself or that other person in such situations; or, just as surprisingly, we are profoundly yet fruitfully in conflict.

There are many other potentially energizing twists that our lives can take as we risk being surprised. Some of these can occur in our musings and fantasies, and some with sharp observation. Some can also arise in books and movies that set our imaginations afire. Yet one of the least appreciated staging grounds for surprise, perhaps, is our pursuit of a personal project. By personal project, I mean any concerted endeavor, such as an art or craft, from which we derive notable and enduring gratification. Periodically—and unpredictably—these projects "transport us," or connect us to other worlds.

Fraser Pierson, for example, experienced this outlook on sustained journeys out to sea. The contours of the waves, the hue of the skies, and the dynamic formations of sea creatures were a continual source of wonder for her, along with a welcoming sense of shock. Charles Gompertz, likewise, courted surprise in his daily chores as a rancher. The shifts of the weather, the changes of season, and the cycles of life all unveiled marvels for him that he would reflect on and savor.

I know many more people who share in this sensibility in the least likely settings. For example, I have a good friend who is a business owner on weekdays and a photographer on weekends. He will work his nine-to-five week dutifully and then descend into his darkroom on Saturdays to create some of the most provocative and sensual photographs around. He will sometimes travel miles to connect with his photographic subjects and will work with them in all their jarring naturalness, posed before elaborate, imaginative sets. This fellow declares unabashedly the value of the spontaneous in his avocation, and feeds upon the creative and zestful results. I know others who work in the most regimented professions, such as medicine, who relish sculpting, painting, and even glassblowing. The art or craft serves as a critical counterbalance for them and opens them to dormant yearnings. For example, they are able to really "let go" in these pastimes and experience uncharted sensations and feelings. Sometimes these experiences appear to unsettle them, but mostly they inspire them, free up their energies for other endeavors, and enhance their affirmation of life.

The readiness for surprise is also evident in people who relish travel, sports, and professional or academic study. It is also evident in alive, contemplative people—period. In any area where there is a chance for something new to emerge, something out of the ordinary, there is a stronger likelihood of experiencing awe. Newness—even when revisiting the past—jolts us out of the sleepwalking mode

---

of life, and abruptly shows us how much bigger and more possible things are than we characteristically believed. The challenge here is not so much to seek novelty, but to recognize its ever-present availability. It would be foolhardy, of course, to obsess over these perpetual availabilities, as we would likely go mad; but our main problem in Western culture is that we are barely aware of them, barely able to follow their intriguing, if not ultimately fulfilling, offerings to us.

Being open to the unpredictable, finally, is like seeing the world—at least for moments—like a child. It is "big mind" in Zen Buddhist literature. For a child, each day is a blank canvas holding untold secrets and delights. It is a waiting paintbrush, a colorful palette, and a beckoning story. To the extent that we can approach these sensibilities and seize upon the "blank canvas" of our day, we can lift ourselves—even partially—out of our entrenched lives. We can "get out of our way" and greet the unexpected along our path; and we can breathe a little freer, a little fuller, wherever we are.

The Lens of Vastness

Here too we meet the cosmosphere, albeit in its most prodigious dimensions. The lens of vastness opens out in infinite directions. The moment I walk outdoors, for example, I engage it. I perceive it in the distances and horizons, in parks, and in wildernesses, in the rolling hills, and amid the daunting bluffs. I connect with it while driving through urban sprawl and while peering into ocean sunsets. But beyond these physical settings, vastness embraces all that we perceive and intuit.

Consider cultural anthropologist Ernest Becker's riff on the "causal chain" of human conception. When asked to discuss "where babies come from," he observed:

> Since we don't know who we are, we don't know how we came here. You don't know where we came from—oh, I know, you say "the sperm and the egg." Sperm and the egg! Where do babies come from? "Sperm and the egg!" Idiot answer. It's not an answer at all, it's merely a de-

scription of a speck in a causal process that is a mystery. We don't know where babies come from. You get married, you're sitting at a table having breakfast—there are two of you—and a year later there's somebody else, sitting there. And if you're honest with yourself, you don't know where they came from. You've made contact with them at the hospital, but that was another step on the causal chain. They just came, literally, out of nowhere, and they keep growing in your environment. If you stop to think about, which you don't, because it's annoying, it's upsetting, then it's a total mystery. And if a child said, "Where did I come from?" you don't know. So you can't answer honestly.[7]

Yet the honest answer, as Becker so deftly notes, is an endless chain, a cascade of events that precede earlier events that can be traced only so far. Is this awe-invoking, or just confounding? For many of us I would guess it's the former—particularly if we take the time to ponder it. Another "honest" answer to the incomprehensibilities of life is the vision that it can inspire. By "vision," I mean a picture or philosophy of life as a whole, not just compartments of life. This picture—eminently illustrated by our contributors—holds the potential to dramatically transform our relationships, our outlooks, and indeed our affect on our worlds. This understanding was captured remarkably by a little appreciated film called *Grand Canyon* (1991), starring Danny Glover and Kevin Klein.[8] The film opens with an ordinary upper-class businessman, Mack (played by Kevin Klein), attending a basketball game at the Los Angeles Forum arena. Following the game, he finds himself stuck in traffic so he chooses an alternative route. This route it turns out leads him into one of the most crime-ridden and impoverished areas of the city—South Central LA—and his difficulties mount from there. As he makes his way through a particularly forbidding neighborhood, his car begins to break down. It's late at night, there are few people around, and he's faced with an increasingly fitful choice—either get out of his car and make a phone call to the local towing service, or stay "safe" in his car and hope against hope that someone will assist him. In little time, he makes the decision to make the phone call and just as he sits back in his car to wait for the anticipated help, he is surrounded by a carload of terrorizing, menacing youths.

Just at the point where these youths appear to be accosting him and stealing his car, a tow truck arrives and the driver, Simon (played by Danny Glover), vigilantly steps between Mack and his harassers. What happens at this point reflects, for me, one of the most eloquent examples of an invitation to an enlarged view of life—and hence awe—recorded on film. Although the scene is fictional, it is rife with real-life implications, and in one of the most challenging circumstances—the inner city. After attempting to calm the situation, Simon turns to his truck and begins preparing his towline. However, superficial gestures will clearly not do in this situation, and the youths, particularly their leader, become increasingly aggravated. Accordingly, the leader steps away from his "home boys" and plants himself squarely in front of Simon. While Mack braces himself near his car, Simon mindfully goes about his duty while keeping a concerted connection with the leader. Finally the leader forces an encounter with Simon, asking, in effect, are you disrespecting me? Simon turns to him, collects his breath and retorts that he's not disrespecting him at all but just trying to do his job. At this point, Simon continues his duties, but the leader, along with his impatient friends, will not relent. He keeps after Simon, and with rising agitation Simon tells him curtly that the towing operation is his responsibility and that if anything—or anyone—disrupts it they put his job at risk. The leader, however, refuses to accept this answer and questions whether Simon is now challenging his intelligence. It is at this point that Simon starts to lose patience with the leader and admits to him that he doesn't know whether he's intelligent but that what he does know is that the leader, along with his gun, is preventing him from carrying out his job.

Now to this point the encounter follows an ordinary, if unusually candid, trajectory: Simon has a job to do and the boy demands respect for letting Simon do that job, and for dashing, as a result, the boy's plans to steal Mack's car. But there is much more at play here, as Simon is no ordinary bystander. One has a feeling about Simon that he deeply relates to the boy, that he had been in his shoes at some point in his past, but that he also will not readily coddle him or accede to his debasing demands. Simon senses that what the boy really needs is not one-upmanship, or the platitudes extracted at the point of a gun, but an honest and enlarged vision of himself and of the possibilities for living.

Hence when the boy replies to Simon that he will "permit" him the favor of yielding to him but only on one condition—that Simon answer whether he is asking the favor out of a "sign of respect" or because of the gun, Simon's retort is concise: "Man, the world ain't supposed to work like this. Maybe you don't know that. I'm supposed to do my job without asking you if I can. That man [Mack] is supposed to be able to wait with his car without you ripping him off. *Everything is supposed to be different than what it is*" [emphasis mine].

Accordingly, the lesson that Simon teaches in my view is that the boy has more of a choice than he realizes. He can continue to pretend that he's powerful by beating people up and brandishing a gun, or he can look to a larger world that allows people to "go on their way," be more of who they are, and feel more for each other.

After Simon and Mack are "permitted" to leave, they sit together at the curb of the gas station where Mack's car is being repaired. This is one of those magical moments of artistry where class and race and even humanity are viewed from above, as it were, which entirely changes their character. Such a situation may or may not happen in reality, but it can deeply inform our reality, and the seeds to reform it.

Simon: You go swimming in the ocean, every day and everything could be cool; but then one day, this one particular day, you bump into the big shark. Now the big shark don't hate you, he has no feeling for you at all—you just look like food to him. . . . Those boys back there, they've got nothing to lose, if you just happen to be swimming along and bump into them, well . . .

Mack: Just seems like so many ways to "buy it." I'm amazed at the end of the day that anybody's alive, especially in this city. Then other days I think maybe people aren't so fragile. Things have always been kind of brutal, and people, they just keep on going.

Simon: You ever been to the Grand Canyon?

Mack: We've always meant to go.

Simon: I was there. . . . Man, get yourself to the Grand Canyon.

Mack: Beautiful, huh?

Simon: Ah, it's pretty alright—but that ain't the thing of it. [What really] got me was sitting on the edge of that big old thing. Those rocks . . . those cliffs, man [they] are so old. It took so long for that thing to look like that. It ain't gone either; it happens right while you're sitting there watching it. . . . While we're sitting here in this ugly town. When you sit on the edge of that thing you just realize what a joke we people are. What big heads we got thinking that what we do is going to matter all that much. . . . It's a split second that we been here, the whole lot of us. And one of us? That's a piece of time too small to give a name.

Mack: You trying to cheer me up?

Simon: Yeah, those rocks are laughing at me. I could tell, me and my worries. It's real humorous to that Grand Canyon. You know what I felt like? I felt like a gnat that lands on the ass of a cow that's chewing its cud next to a road that you ride by on at seventy miles an hour.

Mack: Small.

Simon: Yeah, it's small.

Mack [reaching out to shake hands]: My name's Mack.

Simon: Simon.

Grand Canyon shows that the lens of vastness can operate at any time, any place. It shows that vastness—awe—is always in the background, both haunting and exhilarating us. The question is, will we dare to "sit by its edge," allow ourselves to be moved by it, and act in accord with its wisdom?

The Lens of Intricacy

In the opening credits of Alfred Hitchcock's cinematic tour de force *Vertigo*, the camera focuses on a distressed yet radiant female face.[9] As the camera zooms in, it frames the woman's darting eyes. In quick succession it zooms directly into one of those eyes and spirals, both literally and figuratively, into its depths. In another scene, a mysterious woman named Madeline (played by Kim Novak) sits in a museum observing the painting of another mysterious woman, Carlotta Valdez. These women are linked by one outstanding trait—spiraling hair buns. As the camera homes in, the spiraling hair buns are played off one another, furthering and deepening their enigmatic linkage.

There is something about the image of spiraling, as Hitchcock so well knew, that both intrigues and unnerves. There is something about spiraling inward that evokes dizzying imbalance—and hence vertigo, in the perceiver. What is that? Is it the spinning movements of the camera, or the designs upon which it focuses? Or is it something in the connotations of inward exploration, methodical revelation? I would estimate both.

The lens of intricacy opens us to the hidden realms of existence. These are the realms of *Vertigo*, but also parallel classics such as *Dracula* (Bram Stoker), *Phantom of the Opera* (Gaston Leroux), and *Fall of the House of Usher* (E. A. Poe). In these works we find mesmerizing tales of underground lairs, secret alliances, and subliminal forces. Each in its own way celebrates the subtleties of life, be those of mind or material. When the "doors of perception" are "cleansed," elucidates Blake, "everything would appear to man as it is, infinite."[10]

But where, in real life—aside from the attestations in this book—can we find similar experiences of microcosmic wonder? How does intricacy beckon us daily? Consider, for example, our friends, relatives, or associates. Do they not possess virtually endless stories of loss or love, rage or joy that transfix us and whet our appetites to know more? Why not ask these folks to elaborate on their backgrounds, or do some investigating on our own? I recently found out, for example, that my paternal grandfather, who died when my father was just five, was a beer-maker in the Red Hook district of Brooklyn in the 1920s—the very same locale that harbored notorious mobsters such as Al Capone. I learned further that this otherwise nondescript and apparently caring father to my dad and uncle appears to have docket numbers in the Brooklyn criminal court! Who knows what subtleties we can learn about our own or others' pasts, unless we investigate them or remain open to their emergence. How many times, for example, do we sit down with elders and ask them to tell their stories, which are generally rife with entanglements. One may learn, for example, of long-simmering rivalries, secret romances, or agonizing failures; one may become privy to untold talents, exuberant adventures, or illuminating discoveries. The point is that, when looked at closely, the composition of lives is a staggering phenomenon, and anyone who braves such an inquiry is likely to feel abundantly rewarded.

The lens of intricacy is also what captivates many of us about meditation and psychotherapy. Not only do these practices deepen and enrich many of us—as we have seen with several of our contributors—they hold the potential to markedly transform our worlds. Consider further, for example, the transformative power of self-inquiry, as wishes, wants, and anxieties are unveiled. As a practitioner of psychotherapy—as well as meditation—I know how energizing these processes can be, as well as jarring. The themes that can come up can range from dizzying dreads to dazzling desires, and from meandering fantasies to timely practicalities. But the overarching effect is that the more that one is informed by such engagements, the greater one's potential for a full and diversified life—a life of depth but also vibrancy. This sensibility can be illustrated by the time that one takes with both people and things. It can be seen in one's attentiveness to one's friends, loved ones, or acquaintances; in one's sensitivity to art, beauty, and nature. When is the last time, for example, that you have attended to the markings on a leaf, or the brusqueness of an autumn wind, or the tenderness of a lover's skin? When have you paused to investigate ant colonies, or the loping grace of a running dog, or the aesthetics of a neighbor's home? How much time do you devote to digging beyond the requirements of a work assignment, or exploring alternative thoughts, philosophies, or lifestyles? When is the last time you experienced the delicacies of a foreign restaurant, culture, or religion? Would you be willing to venture into a mosque or temple or church; or open yourself to the sacraments of these structures and the rituals they harbor? What if more religious groups actually hosted such interchanges: Would this not broaden and inspire as well as unsettle and challenge? Would this not bring a renewed appreciation for the complexities of peoples' lives, the significance and subtleties that are so often denied, dismissed, and contorted? These and so much more are the potentialities inherent as the lenses of intricacy are polished.

The Lens of Sentiment

The experience of emotion and of being profoundly moved are the key features of this lens. Sentiment offers us a deepened sensibility, a refined feeling, toward both people and things, life and art. The question for this lens is to what extent we can "drop in" to it as exemplified by our responses to love and to loss, to beauty and to repulsion, or to any momentary encounter. How and in what ways can we linger over those sensibilities, take them in, and allow them to shake us to our core? For example, to what extent can we stand before beauty—like Fraser Pierson or Jeff Schneider, or many of the elders in our volume—and allow our breath to be taken away? Can we permit this on our walk outside on a spring day; or in the face of a ravishing woman or man; or how about in the presence of a haunting melody? Peggy Salkind, an accomplished teacher and pianist, as well as octogenarian, opines on the latter:

> Music . . . is a reservoir of feeling and contains the ultimate distillation of love. It is a refuge for all the most trenchant sensibilities of the human heart. Music can change a person's consciousness without the use of drugs. It establishes an incontrovertible bond between psyche and soma. Music is a language without limits in that all who hear it can share in its wonders without possessing linguistic skills. Music subsumes sex and lasts longer. It endures for a lifetime and becomes a haven of peace and renewal for each individual who undertakes the task of exploring its mysteries. Human beings need to explore every possible avenue in an effort to cope with the beauty and terror of existence. Music is a viable means of engaging that exploration. After all . . . language alone cannot express the sum total of any human being. Music is the true transubstantiation. Through it human essence is transformed into universal divinity.[11]

As the passage above implies, virtually any emotion can bring us in touch with the largeness of life—love, joy, and exuberance to be sure, but even fear, anger, and sorrow. For example, while love and joy can evoke sensuality and celebration, fear can evoke curiosity, sharpened attunement, and a humbling respect. Anger, correspondingly, can apprise us of our passion, tenacity, and capacity to reform; and sorrow can alert us to the depth and urgency of our lives—and to the peril contrastingly, when that depth and urgency are ignored.

The great question, of course, is how to negotiate these varying sentiments without being overtaken by them, without overidentifying with their demonic potentials. By "demonic" here, I mean the potential for any singular sentiment to take over one's entire personality, and thereby to squelch awe. Awe can only be fostered to the degree that *both* wonder and humility, boldness and respectfulness, can be present; to the degree they are absent, one's vision is truncated.[12] This truncation is exemplified by joy that forgets the fleeting nature of time, or fear that neglects adventurousness, or anger that misses tenderness, or sorrow that overlooks possibility, and so on. The point here is that there is a significant difference between "tapping into" the lens of sentiment and being "locked" there, or between being mobile in one's relations to feeling and being paralyzed. This perspective then advocates for a mobility in one's relations with sentiment, and for the patience, practice, and training that can support such a capacity.

The Lens of Solitude

This is one of the essential, yet least celebrated, lenses for awe. It may also be a prerequisite for the other lenses. To be sure, solitude is a state of aloneness; but it is also, as many in this book have testified, a state of aliveness, attentiveness, and absorption. Solitude can be isolating but it is not generally alienating; to the contrary, it is frequently renewing, deepening, and strengthening. In this era of cell phones and instant messaging, solitude can clear a space for what really matters in one's life and for how to pursue what really matters. By encouraging us to step back, take a breath, and stay acutely present, solitude opens the way to multiple expressions of awe.

One can see the foundational value of solitude for virtually any relationship, be that with oneself, others, or the world about one. To the degree that one can stay present to and coexist with oneself, one is in a much improved position to stay present to and coexist with all that surrounds one—such as creation's transience, mystery, surprise, vastness, intricacy, poignancy, and in short, awe.

To this end, it is helpful to be alone once in awhile, and to unplug from the hubbub of life. It is also helpful to take solitary walks periodically, or to retreat to one's office, garden, or hobby. Or it can also be restorative—as well as awe-inspiring—to reserve places to meditate or write or observe, or to just simply "be." Being, ironically, is accorded an extraordinarily lowly status in our Western society, and, increasingly, the world. And yet being—the capacity to simply attend to and witness living—can spark a radically transformative state.

Who among us, for example, has not appreciated, at some level, the exquisiteness of our time alone? The luminous poet Rumi has characterized this exquisiteness as a "guest house" in which a legion of "visitors" flows in and out. While these characters are sometimes rough, and sometimes bitter, they all can take us beyond ourselves, and even beyond our imagining. This beyond can be awe-inspiring, Rumi implies, if only we would take time to "greet" it.[13] Thomas Merton also appreciated the delicacies of solitude, albeit in a most stringent form. Although Merton was a monk, his wise words about the "solitary" evoke collective awe:

> The solitary life is full of paradoxes: the solitary is at peace, but not as the world understands peace, happy but not in the worldly sense of a good time, going but unsure of the way, not knowing the way but arriving. . . . The solitary possess all riches but of emptiness, embracing interior poverty but not of any possession. The solitary has so many

riches he cannot see God, so close to God that there is no perspective or object, so swallowed up in God that there is nothing left to see.

"This realization of one's solitude," Merton concludes, is "the only way to find others, to have compassion for others, [and] to see the common humanity of all."[14]

THE SOCIETAL
CHALLENGE

As we have now demonstrated, not only is the cultivation of awe a boon to personal well-being, it has significance for humanity. In this light, the ethical implications of cultivating awe can hardly be overstated. For example, the general conditions favorable to such cultivation—presence, freedom, courage, and appreciation—echo incisively the general conditions favorable to the democratic principles of community. Among these are the right to deliberation, the tolerance for interpersonal differences, and the right to liberty (e.g., independence, choice). Put another way, to the extent that one can be present, free, courageous, and appreciative, one can meet the major challenges for democracy; to the extent that one shrinks from the awe-based conditions, one jeopardizes the democratic stance. To be sure, the democratic stance is not universally embraced—totalitarian regimes, for example, reject it outright. However, for an emerging cross-section of humanity, democracy and the awe-based sensibilities on which it is based are sacrosanct, and this goes for religious and secular alike.

AWE AND THE DEMOCRATIC CHARACTER:
A DEEPENING BOND

As a seed of democracy, awe venerates the whole of life, both within and without. It prizes inquiry, passion, and diversity, along with the natural beauty of creation. At the same time, however, awe recognizes ambiguities in its purview—such as instabilities, discomforts, and puzzlements. It prizes openness but at the same time acknowledges overwhelmingness, adventurousness, but also human frailty and the cost of forsaking that frailty. To this degree, awe points modern democracies toward depth. Although this depth was nascent in the founding spirit of the U.S. Constitution with its call, for example, for equal protection, as well as equal treatment, it was not until recently that such equality and its associated challenges—such as minority and gender rights—was substantively addressed. In the ensuing years, these social perplexities have only multiplied, and the demands to deal with them have magnified. The question now, therefore, is not only how we consolidate the principles of freedom and responsibility—equality and protection—for society, but whether we are willing to take the next logical step and apply them to people's intimate, moment-to-moment encounters? It is one thing, for example, for a person to experience equality at the level of a voting booth or paycheck, but quite another for him or her to experience it (or its underlying "fellow feeling") at the company watercooler, or at the health club, or community recreation center. And even beyond these subtler applications of democracy, where is the place for the experience of equality—or its correlates, inclusion and confirmation—in the design of one's education, work setting, or place of worship? What about in relationships with friends, family, or even community leaders? To what extent can these be infused with the openness and attunement, aliveness and significance of the institutional expressions of democracy?

These are the questions we can and now must pose if we are to move beyond pat formulas and simple slogans espousing collective liberty. Again, these "bromides" were critical in their time, but as people's needs grow for a more personally meaningful, vocationally fulfilling life, that time is waning. In short, the movement toward a new democratic character structure, not just society, is upon us, and this character structure points to depth of living, not merely breadth of opportunities.

How then can awe inform people "on the ground," so to speak, about how "best"—and I use this term advisedly because I am mindful of its plasticity—to treat each other? What have we learned from our analysis to help with person-to-person dialogue, for example, or intercultural exchange? To consider these questions at some length, we need to turn to the specific lenses or tools for awe cultivation detailed in the section above. These lenses, in other words, can help us to open to the subtleties of the democratic process—or what Arnie Mindell has called "deep democracy"[1] and what I shall term momentarily "experiential democracy." By deep democracy, Mindell means a democracy that is personal and sometimes even intimate. It is a democracy of one's relation to oneself as well as to others, and it is a sensitizing to the vast potentialities—as well as perils—of an enlarged global consciousness. This is a consciousness with a radically transformed capacity to deliberate decisions of major ethical import; to form creative responses in the face of that deliberation; and to optimize consensus on the basis of these processes. This is also a consciousness that stresses *experiential* encounter with whomever and whatever dwells before one. By experiential, I mean encounter that is both mindful and embodied, immediate and attuned.

Let us look more closely now at how the lenses of awe might assist. Consider, for example, the lens of transience: How would people treat each other if they realized their passing natures? How would an employer treat an aging employee if he was acutely aware of his own fragility? How would the employee feel as the recipient of this sensibility? How would parents respond to their children if they prized their children's growth process? What kind of priorities (e.g., in terms of work and home life, physical and emotional contact, depth of interaction) would these parents stress, and how might those priorities shift? What about those who view friendship or romance through the lens of transience? To what extent would their connections intensify, their conversations deepen, and their interpersonal attunements sharpen? What about the encounter with those of diverse backgrounds—classes, cultures, races? How would the awareness of transience impact peoples' respective abilities to appreciate one another, to value the uniqueness of the moment, and to recognize the opportunity for worldly discovery?

What about the lens of unknowing? To what extent would this lens inspire people to stay present to each other and to attune to the unfolding dimensions that can be shared with each other? To what extent would it give people hope who would otherwise despair, or a sense of mutual adventure and accompaniment? Correlatively, how might surprise color our worlds—the openness to spontaneous expression or mutual discovery; the risk to trust, even when that trust is founded less on custom or even past experience, but on careful intuitive observation? Consider what such openness could bring to the problems of clashing races or battling ideologies; or how about the discoveries of new ways to look at and treat each other, as well as the land and existence around us?

What of the lens of vastness—what uplift might it provide? How might it affect our capacity to see beyond circumscribed fears or transient hurts? What could it provide in the way of long- versus short-term thinking, wider vision, and sturdier personality? How might it help with faith and emotional refuge, self-esteem and inner strength? How about the esteem or strength conferred on others (as in the example provided by Simon in *Grand Canyon*)?

What of intricacy and its spin-offs? How might intricacy deepen our ability to discover ourselves, as well as those around us? How might it sensitize us to nature and to the needs of nature? What about its implications for "reading between the lines" in complex or tension-filled relationships, or attunement to individual circumstances in multilayered ethical dilemmas (such as in the decision to participate in war, or to abort one's fetus)?

What about the capacity for sentiment? To what extent would attunement to emotions help us to understand one another, or to sensitively approach the world about us? How might sentiment figure into our creation of laws and rules, as well as our prizing of unique person-to-person situations (such as the calls of conscience, the desire for individual expression, or the need to consider circumstances)?

Finally, what of the lens of solitude in the formation of ethical decision-making? To what extent would it help people to exercise their choice to be alone more, to pause, and to "digest" pivotal deliberations? To what degree would solitude facilitate more nuanced decision-making, decision-making forged from the convection currents of time, largeness of view, and internal searching?

In short, to what extent can awe help to bring about an enriched consciousness to humanity? This would be a consciousness that will not always "get it right" or provide definitive solutions, but that will support our best efforts, with the fullest, most sensitive instruments about which we know—our own beings.

THE EXPERIENTIAL DEMOCRACY PROJECT

What follows is one example of an application of awe-based democratic principles that may foster the process of world awakening. Two years ago, I embarked on a project to translate and apply awe-based principles of presence, freedom, courage, and appreciation to the legislative arena. My rationale for this ambitious undertaking was—and continues to be—the special interest-driven, ideologically laden debacle that has become, in my and many others' opinions, modern legislative deliberation. The core idea of the Experiential Democracy Project, as I call it, is to supplement the bureaucratically heavy legislative system with a personal or "experiential" component that should, in theory, provide a counterbalance to what is now a very one-sided and too often one-dimensional process.

The experiential democracy component, in other words, can serve as a close-up and personal "check" on a system that too often lacks such checks and that proceeds in reactive haste. This check, moreover, is one critical step, in my view, toward the deep or awe-based democratic vision outlined above. Below is my outline of the project that I am currently proposing to select governmental bodies (i.e., state and national legislatures). My hope is that, particularly with our new president's emphasis on dialogue, some governmental agencies will opt to study this project—and to fathom its merit.[2]

Preamble (drafted in January 2008)

Our legislative process is disabled. It seems that "voting one's conscience," a cornerstone of the democratic spirit of deliberation, has too often given way to voting to stay elected, or to appease vested interests, or to attain the "quick fix." In this light, and as a psychologist schooled in interpersonal mediation, I propose a new direction in the way we think about governance. This is a direction that recharges our system of checks and balances with a new check—*experientially based* deliberation.

Experientially based deliberation—or "experiential democracy" for short—is a "here and now," personally oriented supplement to standardized legislative proceeding. Put another way, it is an opportunity for intensive reflection about an issue of moral import and for the maximization of consensus through empathy. Experiential deliberation is not intended to dominate but to supplement governmental decision-making; it is an attempt to ensure integrity, both within and among deliberators. Here, then, is a brief synopsis of the structure of this proposal:

Proposal Structure

I. Participation in this initial stage of the experiential democracy project is voluntary. Participants are to consist of two diversely opinionated legislators; one legislator observer from each of the two "camps"; an experientially oriented, depth facilitator (e.g., a psychologist trained extensively in experiential and depth approaches with both individuals and groups); and a recording secretary. The meeting is to take place in a private and undistracted setting within the legislative offices.

II. A once weekly (four-week) pilot project entailing the facilitation of the encounter between two diversely opinionated legislators, as described above, during the course of a legislative session.

The time period for the meeting could range between one and two hours (with a preference for two).

a) The legislators would be presented with one or two morally significant, live (or active) agenda items by the facilitator. These items will have been agreed upon in advance by the legislators assembled. Facilitation of the initial pilot study (i.e., meeting) would be initially coordinated by me—although eventually, and if viable, by others.

b) Maintenance of strict confidentiality. The confidentiality of the meeting is sacrosanct. No public disclosure of relational processes (short of breaking the law) would be permitted, and there would be strong sanctions for noncompliance. Media could be invited to the post-small group discussion (e.g., with the full committee or legislative body at large), but not to the meeting itself.

III. The meeting would address the following basic questions/structure:

a) What deeply matters about the (given) agenda item for each party—and not just intellectually or politically, but also personally, in terms of the particular legislator's heartfelt perspective? (Each party would be afforded five minutes to "tell her/his side of the story" as mindfully as possible to the opposing party. The opposing party would then be asked to reflect back what she/he heard from their counterpart, and the counterpart would have a chance to correct that understanding. The roles would then be reversed.)

b) The interaction would then proceed to a deepening of or elaboration on the responses (thoughts and feelings) that have emerged from the earlier disclosures.

c) Next, each party would be asked to declare the important meanings or understandings that have emerged from the dialogue, and how or whether their opinions of the legislation have changed as a result.

d) Finally, each party would consider whether a consensus has been achieved (in which case it would be specifically identified), or has not been achieved (in which case the parties would identify the steps necessary to achieve it). A recording secretary (or observer) would then summarize the results. *The results would be written in a form that strictly prohibits the disclosure of personal details (e.g., emotions, thoughts) of either party, and would focus solely on the conclusions regarding the given agenda item.*

e) The findings would then be brought back to the entire group of legislators (e.g., subcommittee) for general discussion and integration into deliberative proceedings.

Note: For those wanting or needing follow-up counseling on emotional issues arising in the groups, I could be available for referrals and/or advice as warranted.

IV. At the end of the four weekly group meetings, a brief assessment could be administered to each deliberator. This assessment could then be used to help determine the utility/viability of the proposed procedure.

CONCLUSION

Awe is an integral dimension of our physical, emotional, and spiritual well-being. Throughout this volume, and based on many testimonies, awe can be characterized as two distinct yet overlapping modes of consciousness—the mode of *wonder* (e.g., allure, fascination, and adventure) and the mode of *unsettlement* (e.g., anxiety, apprehension, and puzzlement). These modes imply two commingling perceptions of the world—the perception of life's accessibility, freedom, and possibilities, and the perception of life's intricacy, vastness, and incomprehensibility.[1]

From the standpoint of the observer, awe is experienced as the humility and wonder—amazement—of any given instant of being alive. It is also experienced as the thrill and anxiety or bigger picture of any given instant of being alive; and it is perceived as the capacity to be profoundly (i.e., bodily, emotionally, and intellectually) moved by any given instant of being alive.[2] (See the Appendix for a guide and elaboration of this point.)

In addition to its capacity to captivate, we have also learned of awe's capacity to heal. Both on a personal and interpersonal level, awe expands perception beyond fixated or parochial divisions, and lifts it to a broader and deeper plane. In so doing, it can transform moods, mind-sets, and motivations. It can inspire the rigid, for example, to taste the robustness of possibility, or the imprudent to appreciate the delicacies of reserve. It can encourage the fearful to explore or the arrogant to defer. It can convert despair into contemplation, and giddiness into rapture. It can deepen, in an instant, that which at first appeared humdrum; and it can temper the most tempestuous heart. In short, awe can mend lives, and it can do so across socioeconomic, ethnic, gender, developmental, and even religious lines. As we've seen in this book, awe can bring a sense of validation where there formerly was estrangement. It can bring a sense that simply because one is, one is valid, and not only valid but privileged (as a participant in an unfathomable journey).

Awe enjoins the world to a new consciousness. This is an earthy, paradoxical consciousness, which fosters neither "pie-in-the-sky" optimism nor "hangdog" pessimism but a dynamic and vital realism that embraces both. Awe shortchanges neither freedom *nor* anxiety, and by so doing invigorates life. This is a life we are increasingly in need of—and can recharge our days.

One final thought: Awe *could*, as James hints in the closing pages of *The Varieties of Religious Experience*, be the long-sought bridge between religion and democracy, humanism and theology. Citing Leuba, James notes: It is "not [so much an absolutistic view of] God," that religions the world over seek, "but life, more life, a larger, richer, more satisfying life";[3] and are these not the shared aims of an awe-informed humanism—a wonder-charged democracy?

And if these assertions hold true, then why not meet together at the bridge? Why not reenvision and rebuild our world?

Appendix

GENERAL AND SPECIFIC CONDITIONS THAT FOSTER (OR DISCOURAGE) AWE

What follows are general and specific conditions that foster and discourage awe-based awakening. These conditions are grounded in the testimony of the contributors to this volume, as well as my own therapeutic and theoretical knowledge.

General conditions that favor awe-based awakening (or the humility and wonder—amazement—of living). In addition to presence, freedom, courage, and appreciation, consider the following:

- A basic capacity to subsist
- The time to reflect
- A capacity to slow down
- A capacity to savor the moment
- A focus on what one loves
- A capacity to see the big picture
- An openness to the mystery of life and being
- An appreciation for the fact of life
- An appreciation of pain as a sometime teacher
- An appreciation of balance (e.g., between one's fragility and resiliency)
- Contemplative time alone
- Contemplative time in natural or non-distracting settings

- Contemplative time with close friends or companions
- In-depth therapy or meditation
- An ability to stay present to and accept the evolving nature of conflict—e.g., to know that "this too shall pass"
- An ability to stay present to and accept the evolving nature of life
- An ability to give oneself over—discerningly—to the ultimately unknowable
- An ability to trust in the ultimately unknowable

General conditions that discourage awe-based awakening (or the humility and wonder—amazement—of living):

- Poverty and deprivation
- Haste
- Rigidity
- Dogma
- Gluttony
- Anarchy
- Self-inflation
- Self-deflation
- The preoccupation with money
- The preoccupation with status
- The preoccupation with consumerism
- A steady diet of junk food, pills, or alcohol
- A steady diet of mind-numbing TV
- An enthrallment with mechanization
- An enthrallment with simple answers
- A compulsion to think positively
- A compulsion to think negatively
- Fixation
- Coercion
- Reductionism
- Polarization

Specific conditions ("lenses") that can enhance awe-based awakening:

- *The lens of transience*—attunement to the passing nature and therefore preciousness of living
- *The lens of unknowing*—recognition of life's mystery and potential for change, adventure
- *The lens of surprise*—openness to life's spontaneity and many-sidedness
- *The lens of vastness*—recognition of life's grandeur and possibility
- *The lens of intricacy*—attunement to the subtleties of the mental and physical world
- *The lens of sentiment*—appreciation of life's poignant emotions; deepening of the capacity to be moved
- *The lens of solitude*—acknowledgment of the restorative nature of aloneness; befriending one's capacity to be

NOTES

PREFACE

1. R. Otto, *The Idea of the Holy* (New York: Oxford University Press, 1923/1958).
2. K. Schneider, *Rediscovery of Awe: Splendor, Mystery, and the Fluid Center of Life* (St. Paul, MN: Paragon House, 2004).

INTRODUCTION

1. P. Tillich, *The Courage to Be* (New Haven, CT: Yale University Press, 1952).
2. K. Schneider, *Rediscovery of Awe: Splendor, Mystery, and the Fluid Center of Life* (St. Paul, MN: Paragon House, 2004). For an elaboration on the therapeutic implications of awe, see K. Schneider, ed., *Existential-Integrative Psychotherapy: Guideposts to the Core of Practice* (New York: Routledge, 2008).
3. K. Armstrong, *A History of God* (New York: Ballantine, 1993), 396–97.
4. E. Becker, *Beyond Alienation: A Philosophy of Education for the Crisis of Democracy* (New York: Brazillier, 1967), 235.

CHAPTER 1

1. This quote is taken partially from the television program *The Outer Limits*, which aired on CBS in the early 1960s. This was still a time when even television programs dared to address the larger picture of life, and to make awe-informed "statements" about the fears and desires of humanity. Here's the full quote from the program's opening narration: "You are about to participate in a great adventure. You are about to experience the awe and mystery that stretches from the inner mind to the outer limits."

A similar version of this passage was published in my article "Rediscovering Awe: A New Front in Humanistic Psychology, Psychotherapy, and Society." *Canadian Journal of Counseling*, vol. 42, p. 67.

2. C. Wallis, "The Science of Happiness," *Time* (January 17, 2005), A1–68.

3. See L. Alloy and L. Abramson, "Depressive Realism: Four Theoretical Perspectives," in *Cognitive Processes in Depression*, ed. L. B. Alloy (New York: Guilford, 1988), 223–65; P. Doskoch, "The Dumb Side of Happiness," *Psychology Today* (September–October 1994); P. Holt, "Against Happiness," *New York Times Magazine* (June 20, 2004); J. Kiersky, "Insight, Self-deception, and Psychosis in Mood Disorders," in *Insight and Psychosis*, eds. X. F. Amador and A. S. David (New York: Oxford University Press, 1998), 91–104; R. Tedeschi and L. Calhoon, *Trauma and Transformation: Growing in the Aftermath of Suffering* (Thousand Oaks, CA: Sage, 1995); and R. Tedeschi and L. Calhoon, "The Post-traumatic Growth Inventory: Measuring the Positive Legacy of Trauma," *Journal of Traumatic Stress* 9 (1996): 455–71.

4. See G. Bodenhausen, G. Kramer, and K. Susser, "Happiness and Stereotypic Thinking in Social Judgment," *Journal of Personality and Social Psychology* 66, no. 4 (1994): 621–32; K. Jamison, *Touched by Fire: Manic-Depressive Illness and the Artistic Temperament* (New York: Free Press, 1993); D. K. Simmonton, *Who Makes History and Why* (New York: Guilford, 1994); Z. Stambor, "Self-reflection May Lead Independently to Creativity, Depression," *American Psychological Association Monitor* 36, no. 13 (June 2005); Tedeschi and Calhoon, "The Post-traumatic Growth Inventory," 455–71.

5. B. Moyers, Harvard Commencement Address, January 30, 2005 (survey based on a 2002 Time-CNN poll).

6. J. Rifkin, *The European Dream* (Los Angeles: Tarcher, 2005), 32.

7. Rifkin, *The European Dream*, 28.

8. J. Payne, "Obesity Spreads across the Atlantic to Europe," *San Francisco Chronicle* (March 16, 2005), A12.

9. For an extraordinary overview of the regulatory lapses in recent U.S. administrations, see N. Klein, *The Shock Doctrine: The Rise of Disaster*

Capitalism (New York: Henry Holt, 2007) and the documentary film *The Corporation*, dirs. M. Achbar and J. Abbott, Big Picture Media Corporation, 2004.

10. For a methodical overview of the U.S. administration's war policies between 2001 and 2008, see B. Woodward, *State of Denial* (New York: Simon & Schuster, 2006); and *The War Within* (New York: Simon & Schuster, 2008).

11. D. Barstow and R. Stein, "Under Bush, a New Age of Prepackaged TV News," *New York Times* (March 13, 2005), 1.

12. Woodward, *State of Denial.*

13. P. Goodman, "A Bailout Plan, but Will It All Work?" *New York Times* (September 20, 2008), 1.

14. R. Warren, *The Purpose-Driven Life: What on Earth Am I Here For?* (Grand Rapids, MI: Zondervan, 2002).

CHAPTER 2

1. S. Keen, "The Heroics of Everyday Life: A Theorist of Death Confronts His Own End," *Psychology Today* (April 1974), 78.

2. Keen, "The Heroics of Everyday Life," 78.

3. Keen, "The Heroics of Everyday Life," 78.

4. E. Becker, *The Everyday Heroics of Living and Dying* (cassette tape recording #29, produced by *Psychology Today* magazine) (New York: Ziff-Davis Publishing Co., 1974); E. Becker, *Denial of Death* (New York: Free Press, 1973), 19.

5. W. Whitman, *Leaves of Grass*, ed. M. Cowley (New York: Penguin, 1855/1976), 145.

6. P. Tillich, *Kierkegaard's Existential Theology,* part 2 (CD recording T577 123, Paul Tillich Compact Disk Collection) (Richmond, VA: Union PSCE, 1963).

7. For an elaboration on this point, see K. Schneider and B. Tong, "Existentialism, Taoism, and Buddhism: Two Views," in *Existential Psychology East-West,* eds. L. Hoffman and M. Yang (Colorado Springs, CO: University of the Rockies Press, 2009).

CHAPTER 3

1. See W. James, *Varieties of Religious Experience: A Study in Human Nature* (New York: Modern Library, 1902/1936). For an elaboration on

James's methodology, and the reflective, phenomenological heritage that he and other originators, such as Edmund Husserl, spawned, see the methodology section of *The Handbook of Humanistic Psychology: Leading Edges in Theory, Research, and Practice,* eds. K. Schneider, J. Bugental, and F. Pierson (Thousand Oaks, CA: Sage Publications, 2001), 227–324.

CHAPTER 4

1. R. May, *The Art of Counseling,* rev. ed. (New York: Gardner Press, 1989).
2. R. May, *The Courage to Create* (New York: Norton, 1975).

CHAPTER 5

1. B. Atkinson, ed., *The Essential Writings of Ralph Waldo Emerson* (New York: The Modern Library), 7.
2. H. Beston, *The Outermost House: A Year of Life on the Great Beach of Cape Cod* (New York: Henry Holt and Company, 1988), 25.
3. See James F. T. Bugental's publications, including the following books: *The Search for Existential Identity: Patient-Therapist Dialogues in Humanistic Psychotherapy* (San Francisco: Jossey-Bass, 1976); *The Art of the Psychotherapist* (New York: Norton, 1987); and *Psychotherapy Isn't What You Think* (Phoenix, AZ: Zeig, Tucker, 1999).
4. See K. Schneider, J. Bugental, and J. Pierson, eds., *The Handbook of Humanistic Psychology: Leading Edges in Theory, Research, and Practice* (Thousand Oaks, CA: Sage, 2001), ch. 40.
5. Colossus was born in the wilds of the Congo in 1966 where he lived with his gorilla family until captured at approximately six months of age. An animal dealer brought the infant gorilla to America. He and his wife fostered Colossus in their home for several years. During that period, Tony (Colossus's first human name) liked to wear pajamas to bed and was the playmate of the couple's grandchild. Although they loved him, Tony eventually grew too big to live with the couple, and they reluctantly sold him to Benson's Wild Animal Farm in New Hampshire. I first met Tony at Benson's where he was housed in a traditional, square zoo cage. He

was twenty-two years old. Zookeepers told stories of entering his cage to wrestle and play with him until he was an adolescent, at which time liability concerns curtailed such intimate physical contact. They continued to scratch his back through the bars but could no longer hug him. He invented amusing, engaging games with the paper Coke cups in which he received his drinking water. Remarkably, Colossus maintained his mental health, sense of humor, and ability to form loving relationships. In the last few years of his life, while living in a state-of-the-art primate habitat at the Cincinnati Zoo, Colossus was the sought-after companion of younger gorillas, especially females; they appeared to recognize him as a "father figure." He was forty years old when he died of complications during a root canal procedure in 2006. I will always imagine Tony as the silverback leader of a gorilla family in the forests of the Republic of the Congo and remember his beautiful face and personality. Search Google for "Colossus, the Gorilla" if you would like to read more about this amazing primate.

6. Atkinson, *Essential Writings of Ralph Waldo Emerson*, 5.

7. Psalm 23:3.

8. M. Buber, *I and Thou* (New York: Scribner, 1970).

9. See T. Tempest Williams, *Desert Quartet: An Erotic Landscape* (New York: Pantheon Books, 1995).

10. I. Yalom, *Staring at the Sun: Overcoming the Terror of Death* (San Francisco: Jossey-Bass, 2008).

11. D. K. Osbon, ed., *Reflections on the Art of Living: A Joseph Campbell Companion* (New York: HarperPerennial, 1991), 22.

12. G. Ehrlich, *John Muir: Nature's Visionary* (Willard, OH: R. R. Donnelley & Sons, 2000), 196.

13. Ehrlich, *John Muir*, 57.

14. Today, a combination of psychotherapy, medication, social service support, family, and self-care may effectively address the collection of cognitive, affective, behavioral, and relationship disturbances that comprise a diagnosis of schizophrenia. I believe my dad's outcome would have been quite different in the twenty-first century.

15. H. Beston, *The Outermost House*, 25.

16. See V. Frankl, *Man's Search for Meaning* (Boston: Beacon Press, 2006).

17. D. K. Osbon, ed., *Reflections on the Art of Living: A Joseph Campbell Companion* (New York: HarperPerennial, 1999), 23.

18. I. Goffman, *Stigma: Notes on the Management of Spoiled Identity* (New York: Simon & Schuster, 1963).

19. J. Hillman, *The Soul's Code: In Search of Character and Calling* (New York: Random House, 1996), 208.

20. S. London, *On Soul, Character and Calling: An Interview with James Hillman*, 1998, September 29, 2008, www.scottlondon.com/interviews/hillman.html, para. 41.

21. J. Bugental, "To Stand in Awe," *The Existential-Humanist* 1 (Spring 1997).

22. D. Moss, "The Roots and Genealogy of Humanistic Psychology," *The Handbook of Humanistic Psychology: Leading Edges in Theory, Research, and Practice*, eds. K. Schneider, J. Bugental, and J. Pierson (Thousand Oaks, CA: Sage, 2001), 5-20.

23. To learn more about J, K, and L pods, the resident pods of the San Juan Islands and Puget Sound, visit the websites for the Whale Museum at www.whale-museum.org or The Center for Whale Research at www.whale research.com.

24. F. Goodlander, "All about Dying," *Cruising World* (October 2008), 34-38.

25. W. Whitman, *Leaves of Grass* (New York: The Modern Library, 1891-1892), 384-86.

26. W. McLaughlin, ed., *The Laws of Nature: Excerpts from the Writings of Ralph Waldo Emerson* (N. Ferrisberg, VT: Heron Dance, 2006).

27. *Full Moon Names and Their Meanings*, Almanac Publishing, 2007, January 4, 2009, www.farmersalmanac.com/full-moon-names.

28. D. Elkins, "Beyond Religion: Toward a Humanistic Spirituality," *The Handbook of Humanistic Psychology: Leading Edges in Theory, Research, and Practice*, eds. K. Schneider, J. Bugental, and J. Pierson (Thousand Oaks, CA: Sage, 2001), 201-12.

29. A. Maslow, *The Farther Reaches of Human Nature* (New York: Penguin Books, 1976), 46.

30. Maslow, *The Farther Reaches of Human Nature*, 47.

31. F. Mish, ed., *Webster's Ninth New Collegiate Dictionary* (Springfield, MA: Merriam-Webster, 1988), 558.

32. J. Frank and J. Frank, *Persuasion and Healing: A Comparative Study of Psychotherapy*, 3rd ed. (Baltimore, MD: Johns Hopkins University Press, 1993).

33. S. Flexner and L. Hauck, eds., *The Random House Dictionary of the English Language*, 2nd ed., unabridged (New York: Random House, 1987), 1628.

34. Elkins, "Beyond Religion," 207–8.

35. J. Maxwell, "Scotland's Sacred Isle," *AARP The Magazine* (November/December 2008), 92–93.

36. J. Suina and L. Smolkin, "The Multicultural Worlds of Pueblo Indian Children's Celebrations," *Journal of American Indian Education*, 34 (Spring 1995), jaie.asu.edu/v34/V34S3mul.htm.

37. I am grateful for David N. Elkins' in-depth, thought-provoking chapter "Beyond Religion: Toward a Humanistic Spirituality," as referenced in note 27. The reader may also wish to access his book, *Beyond Religion: A Personal Program for Building a Spiritual Life Outside the Walls of Traditional Religion* (Wheaton, IL: Quest Books, 1998).

38. J. Bugental, *The Art of the Psychotherapist* (New York: Norton, 1987), 4.

39. J. Bugental, *Psychotherapy Isn't What You Think* (Phoenix, AZ: Zeig, Tucker, 1999), 52.

40. D. Ackerman, *Deep Play* (New York: Random House, 1999), 12–13.

41. World Wildlife Fund (WWF) is a multinational conservation organization. To learn more, go to its website at www.worldwildlife.org.

42. A. Schweitzer, "Reverence for Life Brings us into a Spiritual Relation with the World," *Christendom*, 1 (1936): 225–39, www1.chapman.edu/schweitzer/sch.reading4.html, sec. II, para. 12.

43. A. Maslow, *The Farther Reaches of Human Nature* (New York: Penguin Books, 1976).

44. Bugental, *The Art of the Psychotherapist*, 4.

45. Maslow, *The Farther Reaches of Human Nature*, 46.

46. Maslow, *The Farther Reaches of Human Nature*, 48.

47. Maslow, *The Farther Reaches of Human Nature*, 48.

48. Mallory B. Lynch, personal communication, October 2008.

49. I. Yalom, *Staring at the Sun: Overcoming the Terror of Death* (San Francisco: Jossey-Bass, 2008), 6.

50. J. Kabat-Zinn, *Full Catastrophe Living: Using the Wisdom of the Body and Mind to Face Stress, Pain, and Illness* (New York: Dell, 1990), 19.

51. V. Frankl, *The Will to Meaning* (New York: New American Library, 1969), 73.

52. Frankl, *The Will to Meaning*, 72.

53. L. Gussman, ed., *Origin for Reverence for Life* (December 21, 1996), www.schweitzer.org/english/aseind.htm.

CHAPTER 6

1. See B. Katie, *Loving What Is: Four Questions That Can Change Your Life* (New York: Three Rivers Press, 2003).

CHAPTER 7

1. J. Borges, *Collected Fictions,* trans. Andrew Hurley (New York: Penguin Books, 1998), 327.

2. U. Betti, *The Burnt Flower-Bed,* trans. H. Reed (London: Samuel French, 1957), 43.

3. W. Shakespeare, *The Tragedy of Macbeth*, Act V, Scene III (New York: Henry Holt, 1889).

4. See Hsinhsinming, *Zen and Zen Classics*, vol. 1, trans. R. H. Blyth (Tokyo: The Hokuseido Press, 1960), p. 64.

5. P. Tillich, *Systematic Theology*, vol. 1 (Chicago: University of Chicago, 1951), 209. Tillich's concept of "New Being," referred to earlier, is also discussed in vol. 1 of *Systematic Theology*; and "Spiritual Presence" is discussed in vol. 3.

CHAPTER 8

1. C. Robertson, "Creativity and Aging: A Study of Creative Older Individuals," Ph.D. diss., Saybrook Graduate School, San Francisco, CA, 1995, 202–8.

PART III

1. V. Frankl, *Man's Search for Meaning* (Boston: Beacon Press, 2006), 50–51.

2. Frankl, *Man's Search for Meaning,* 51.

3. Frankl, *Man's Search for Meaning,* 51.

CHAPTER 10

1. My own term, not to be confused with the Kansas City "Cosmosphere," which is a museum and tour gallery.

2. H. Gardner, *Multiple Intelligences: New Horizons* (New York: Basic Books, 2006), 20–21.

3. V. Woolf, *To the Lighthouse.*

4. R. Serling, director, "The Fear," *Twilight Zone*, CBS television (May 29, 1964).

5. Excerpt from R. Mamoulian, director, *Dr. Jekyll and Mr. Hyde*, courtesy granted by Turner Entertainment Co. (1932). For an elaboration on the power of mystery in classic horror books and films, see K. Schneider, *Horror and the Holy: Wisdom-Teachings of the Monster Tale* (Chicago: Open Court, 1993).

6. The quote is: "The blocking of one's capacity for wonder and the loss of the capacity to experience mystery can have serious effects upon our psychological health." From R. May, "The Loss of Wonder," *Dialogues: Therapeutic Applications of Existential Philosophy,* vol. 1 (Alameda, CA: California School of Professional Psychology Student Publication), 5.

7. E. Becker, "Growing up Rugged: Fritz Perls and Gestalt Therapy," *Revision* 5, no. 2 (1982): 6–14.

8. R. Kasdan, director, *Grand Canyon*, Twentieth Century Fox, USA (1991).

9. A. Hitchcock, director, *Vertigo*, Universal Pictures, USA (1958).

10. W. Blake, *Selected Poetry* (New York: Penguin, 1998), 73. For a fuller discussion of this concept and the stories noted in this paragraph, see K. Schneider, *Horror and the Holy: Wisdom-Teachings of the Monster Tale* (Chicago: Open Court, 1993).

11. P. Salkind, personal communication, 1999.

12. See R. May, *Love and Will* (New York: Norton, 1969) on the distinction between the "demonic" and the "daimonic."

13. Rumi, *The Essential Rumi*, trans. C. Barks (New York: HarperCollins, 1995), 109. For a rich overview of the solitude literature, see H. Thoreau's classic *Walden* (New York: Peebles Press International, n.d.); A. Storr, *Solitude: A Return to the Self* (New York: Free Press, 1988); and C. Moustakas, *Loneliness* (Englewood Cliffs, NJ: Prentice Hall, 1961).

14. Thomas Merton, "Notes for a Philosophy of Solitude," *Disputed Questions* (New York: Farrar, Straus & Cudahy, 1960), 177–207.

CHAPTER 11

1. A. Mindell, *The Deep Democracy of Open Forums: How to Transform Communities* (Charlottesville, VA: Hampton Roads, 2002).

2. I am currently in discussions with a state legislator about the potential implementation of this pilot project.

CONCLUSION

1. For an elaboration on the phenomenon of awe and its close relations, "wonder" and "astonishment," see R. Otto on the mysterious yet fascinating experience of creation in *The Idea of the Holy* (New York: Oxford University Press, 1923/1958), 12; G. Marcel on the *Mystery of Being* (Chicago: Henry Regnery, 1960); M. Heidegger on "Poetically Man Dwells" in *Poetry, Language, Thought,* trans. A. Hofstadter (New York: Harper & Row, 1971), 213–29; A. Heschel on "radical amazement" in *Man Is Not Alone: A Philosophy of Religion* (New York: Farrar, Straus & Giroux, 1951), 11; W. James on the encounter with "the more" in *The Varieties of Religious Experience: A Study in Human Nature* (New York: Modern Library, 1902/1936), 501; and J. Haidt on the two "conditions" of awe: "vastness" and lack of assimilability in *The Happiness Hypothesis: Finding Modern Truth in Ancient Wisdom* (New York: Basic Books, 2006), 203. While each of these works captures critical aspects of the experience of awe—and many that dovetail with the present study—they are also delimited in certain key respects. The first four are delimited by their philosophical over and above empirical emphases; the last is confined by its stress on quantitative (as distinct from in-depth qualitative) research, and all six delimit themselves to overridingly individual over and above societal implications of awe. While the present study is also delimited in key respects—as has been enumerated, it has also taken pains to unveil the richness, the broad and deep applicability of the awe-informed life. To the extent that "scientific psychology [has] had almost nothing to say about awe" (Haidt, *The Happiness Hypothesis*, 202), the present study provides a counterweight. But what is even more important, in my view, is that the present study helps to counter our awe-depleted mentality, both within and beyond science.

2. For a superb exploration of "the experience of being deeply moved" and its implications for awe, see A. Millay Shepperd, "The Experience of Being Deeply Moved: A Qualitative Study," Ph.D. diss., Institute of Transpersonal Psychology, Palo Alto, CA, 2006.

3. Cited in James, *The Varieties of Religious Experience*, 497. The conclusions reached in this passage not only challenge the polarization of religion

against democracy, but also, and most fashionably, the polarization of democracy (science, humanism, etc.) against religion (e.g., see S. Harris, *The End of Faith: Terror and the Future of Reason* [New York: Norton, 2004]; and D. Dennett, *Breaking the Spell: Religion as a Natural Phenomenon* [New York: Viking, 2006]). Like Freud before them, for example, in *The Future of an Illusion*, these writers identify acutely the problem with simplistic and dogmatic doctrines; however, they miss the boat entirely, in my view, when it comes to the life-affirming essence of many of these doctrines. Consider, for example, the humanitarian and indeed awe-based influences of Jewish philosopher Abraham Heschel, Hindu sage Mahatma Gandhi, and Christian visionary Martin Luther King. It is upon these latter foundations that a religion and democracy can thrive.

INDEX

experiential democracy: defining, 173; project for, 175–78

faith, 104
The Fall of the House of Usher (Poe), 3, 165
Father Knows Best (television series), 71
fetishization, 57
financial collapse, 14, 133
Fowler, Jim, 71
Frankenstein (film), 3
Frankl, Viktor, 41, 81, 148, 153
Fredericks, Frankie, 142
freedom: creativity and, 29; as expediency, 14–15; happiness and, 14–15; as inner condition, 15–16; multifaceted nature of, 16; presence and, 148
Freedom and Destiny (May), 33
freethinking, 138
Freud, Sigmund, 195n3
Frost, Robert, 118
functional environments, 40–41
fundamentalism, 103, 104

Galileo, 132
Gandhi, 95, 195n3
Gardner, Howard, 152
global warming, 13, 89
Glover, Danny, 161–62
God: Cooper on, 103–4; Hernandez exploration of concept of, 32–33
Goffman, Irving, 74
Golden Rule, 56–57
Gompertz, Charles, 22, 121, 159; awe defined by, 125–27; on basis for sense of awe, 127–28;

on healing and awe, 128–30; on professional role of awe, 130–32; on religion and awe, 133–35; on society and awe, 132–35, 133–35
Goodlander, Fatty, 76
Grand Canyon (film), 161–64, 174
Great Depression, 14

Haidt, J., 194n1
Hamlet (Shakespeare), 154
The Handbook of Humanistic Psychology (Bugental; Pierson, J. F.; and Schneider, K.), 62
happiness, 194n1; depth v., 12–15; as engagement, 14; false, 16; freedom and, 14–15; normalcy and, 13; religious beliefs and, 15–16
The Happiness Hypothesis: Finding Modern Truth in Ancient Wisdom (Haidt), 194n1
harmony, 20
healing: awe and, 31–32, 68–74, 85–86, 90, 114–19, 128–30, 179–80; life stages and, 73–74
helplessness, 32
Hernandez, Jim, xii, 22, 27, 48, 147, 149, 155; awe-based culture class developed by, 28–30, 36–38, 37, 48–51; awe defined by, 30–31; awe stirring, 35–36; on creating functional environments, 40–41; on expansion, 41; God explored by, 32–33; on human nature, 38–40, 47; on importance of awe, 46–48; Marshall and, 29–30;

Tillich, Paul, 88, 117, 118, 119
Time (magazine), 12
To Kill a Mockingbird (film), 3
tolerance, 16, 53, 148
To the Lighthouse (Woolf), 154
transcendence, 62, 157
transience, 153–55, 173–74, 183
transpersonal, 75
trauma, childhood, 61
trust: in human nature, 47; in nature, 46–47
truth, 19, 75
The Twilight Zone (television series), 3, 155

unknowing, 155–57, 157, 174, 183
unsettlement, 179
U.S. Constitution, 172

van der Ryn, Julia, 22, 51
Van Gogh, Vincent, 140
The Varieties of Religious Experience (James), 22, 180
vastness, 160–64, 174, 183, 194n1
Vertigo (film), 164–65
violence prevention, 36

"The Vital Lie" (Becker), 145

Waddle, Dave, 144
Walt Disney Presents, 71
Warren, Rick, 15
West Side Story (play), 145
What I Believe (Einstein), 1
Whitman, Walt, 64, 76–77
Wild Kingdom (television series), 71
The Wizard of Oz (film), 3, 76
wonder, 179, 194n1
Woods, Phil, 137, 141
Woods Hole Oceanographic Institution, 72
Woolf, Virginia, 154
World Wildlife Fund, 79
A Wrinkle in Time, 3
writing, 49
Wylie, Philip, 116

Yalom, Irvin, 80
Yes, 141
"You Make Me Feel So Young" (Sinatra), 141
youth violence prevention, 28
Yunus, Muhammad, 133

ABOUT THE AUTHOR

Kirk J. Schneider, Ph.D., is a licensed psychologist and leading spokesperson for contemporary humanistic psychology. Dr. Schneider is current editor of the *Journal of Humanistic Psychology*, vice president of the Existential-Humanistic Institute (EHI), and adjunct faculty at Saybrook Graduate School, the California Institute of Integral Studies, and the Institute for Transpersonal Psychology. He is also a Fellow of three Divisions of the American Psychological Association (Humanistic, Clinical, and Independent Practice).

Dr. Schneider has published more than one hundred articles and chapters and has authored or edited eight books, including *The Paradoxical Self: Toward an Understanding of Our Contradictory Nature*; *Horror and the Holy: Wisdom-teachings of the Monster Tale*; *The Psychology of Existence: An Integrative, Clinical Perspective* coauthored with Rollo May; *The Handbook of Humanistic Psychology: Leading Edges in Theory, Research and Practice* coauthored with J. Bugental and F. Pierson; *Rediscovery of Awe: Splendor, Mystery, and the Fluid Center of Life*; and *Existential-Integrative Psychotherapy: Guideposts to the Core of Practice*. Dr. Schneider is the 2004 recipient of the Rollo May award for "outstanding and independent pursuit of new frontiers in humanistic psychology" from the Humanistic Psychology Division of the American Psychological Association

(APA). Most recently, Dr. Schneider conducted existential-humanistic therapy for an APA video series on psychotherapy called "Psychotherapy Over Time" (see www.apa.org/videos) and with Orah Krug completed *Existential-Humanistic Therapy* for the American Psychological Association monograph series, due to be published in fall 2009. For further information about Kirk Schneider's work, visit his website at www.kirkjschneider.com.